FROM
STANDARDS
TO **RUBRICS** IN
6 STEPS

Dedication

*For the many educators who create quality assessments
for their students and graciously share their work with others.*

KAY BURKE

FROM
STANDARDS
TO RUBRICS IN
6 STEPS

Tools for Assessing
Student Learning, K-8

CORWIN PRESS
A SAGE Publications Company
Thousand Oaks, California

For information:

 Corwin Press
A Sage Publications Company
2455 Teller Road
Thousand Oaks, California 91320
www.corwinpress.com

Sage Publications Ltd.
1 Oliver's Yard
55 City Road
London, EC1Y 1SP
United Kingdom

Sage Publications India Pvt. Ltd.
B-42, Panchsheel Enclave
Post Box 4109
New Delhi 110 017 India

Printed in the United States of America

Library of Congress Cataloging-in-Publication Data

Burke, Kay.
From standards to rubrics in six steps: Tools for assessing student learning, K–8/Kay Burke.
      p. cm.
Includes bibliographical references and index.
ISBN–1-4129-1778-6 or 978-1-4129-1778-0 (cloth)
ISBN–1-4129-1779-4 or 978-1-4129-1779-7 (pbk.)
   1. Competency based education. 2. Curriculum planning. 3. Educational tests and measurements.
4. Grading and marking (Students) 5. Education, Elementary—Curricula—United States. I. Title.
LC1032.B87 2006
372.126′4—dc22   2005029176

This book is printed on acid-free paper.

      07 08 09 10 9 8 7 6 5 4 3

Acquisitions Editor:	Jean Ward
Editorial Assistant:	Jordan Barbakow
Production Editor:	Beth A. Bernstein
Copy Editor:	David Yurkovich
Typesetter:	C&M Digitals (P) Ltd.
Proofreader:	Dennis W. Webb
Indexer:	Sylvia Coates
Cover Designer:	Rose Storey

CONTENTS

ACKNOWLEDGMENTS

I would like to thank Douglas Rife, the CEO of Corwin Press, for welcoming the former SkyLight authors into the Corwin family. It is an honor to be associated with a publishing company committed to providing quality professional development for educators.

It has been a privilege to work with so many dedicated educators in my workshops throughout the country. I would especially like to thank Iris Moran, Area Superintendent of the Tri-Cities Cluster in Fulton County, Georgia, who led an initiative to train principals and teachers in authentic assessment and differentiated learning. Collaborating with Ms. Moran and these exceptional principals and teachers has been the highlight of my professional career.

I would also like to thank the following district leaders and teachers for graciously allowing me to share their work in this book:

Juanita Nelson, principal, and Jacinta Alexander, Jacqueline Burns, LaTrece Crane, and Lydia Rice at Hapeville Elementary School in the Tri-Cities Cluster of Fulton County, Georgia;

Serena Lowe, principal, and Cynthia Bennett, Martha Williams, and Montreal Gore at Conley Hills Elementary School in the Tri-Cities Cluster of Fulton County, Georgia;

Dr. Noris Price, principal of Woodland Charter School, and Elaine Bolton, Margaret Breiner, Robyn Brown, Katie Byrd, Wendy Lea, Anita Lindsley, and Mae Maddox, members of the Assessment Cadre funded by a grant from the Georgia Department of Education Charter School Division and sponsored by the principals and teachers of the North Springs Cluster of Fulton County, Georgia;

Dr. Julie Davis, Director SAIL for EDUCATION, Hal Hixson and educators attending workshops sponsored by Central Ohio Regional School Improvement Team (COSIT); Marguerethe Jaede and Sharon Sims from Columbus Public Schools; Brian House, Scotty McGraner, Brook Yoder, Courtney Potts, and Elizabeth Ratliff of Marysville Exempted Village Schools, and Julia Barthelmes and Laura Tucker from Dublin City Schools in Ohio;

Cheryl Love, Director of Professional Learning, and Krista L. Drescher, Gillian B. Conner, LaTanja M. Harris, June Ladson, LaSonya M. Magee, Lara McMahan, Brenda Avery, Janice Alvarez, Gloria Winslow Smith, Christopher Chambers, and Dr. Teri Williams from DeKalb County Schools in Decatur, Georgia;

Gwenda Rotton, Director of Vocational Education and Personnel, and Robin Goodman and Cheryl Cobb of Metter Elementary School and Jessica F. Brown of Metter Intermediate School in Candler County, Georgia;

Li Massey, Director of Professional Development, and Concetta Archer, Ron Ullman, Susan Wiba, Michele Hoglund, Marily Hall, Debbie Rhodes, Sherree Hatcher, Rosa Patterson, Roslyn Tymes, Dawn Harper, Beth Johnson, Kerri Deal. Beth Hendrickson, Patrica Horner, and Janine R. Shingle with Muscogee County Schools in Columbus, Georgia;

Chris Jaeggi, editor and consultant, Arlington Heights, Illinois; and

Eileen Depka, Supervisor of Standards and Assessment, School District of Waukesha, Wisconsin.

I would like to thank all the members of the Brown and Burke families, my husband Frank Burke, Susan Gray, Donna Ramirez, Ron Nash, Richie Wood, Pat Jackson, Nancy Larimer, Cheryl Hungerford, Andrew Smith, Maureen Wheeler, Patsy Clark, Diane Ray, Rhonda Baldwin, Robin Fogarty, and many others for their encouragement and support. I would also like to thank Jean Ward, Beth Bernstein, Hudson Perigo, and the staff at Corwin Press for their patience and expertise throughout this two-year writing process.

It has taken many steps and several missteps to finally arrive at this Six-Step book. I am truly grateful to my friends, colleagues, and workshop participants who have made this journey with me.

ABOUT THE AUTHOR

 **Kay Burke** has taught at the high school and university levels and served as department chairperson, dean of students, mentor, and administrator. Her dissertation at Georgia State University in 1986 focused on standardized testing. For the past 16 years, Dr. Burke has delivered keynote addresses, written books and training manuals, and worked throughout the United States, Canada, and Australia to provide professional development for educators. Her areas of expertise include standards-based performance assessment; student, teacher, and administrative portfolios; classroom management; and mentoring.

She is a strong advocate of the balanced assessment model where students demonstrate their knowledge, skills, and conceptual understanding through a repertoire of methods like teacher-made tests and quizzes, portfolio work samples, performances, and projects.

Currently, she is an independent author/consultant working with state departments of education, districts, and schools to create curriculum units, organizational checklists, and rubrics all correlated to state standards. Kay is the editor of *Mentoring Guidebook Level I: Starting the Journey* (2nd ed.) and *Mentoring Guidebook Level 2: Exploring Teaching Strategies;* she is coauthor of *The Portfolio Connection: Student Work Linked to Standards* (2nd ed.), and author of the books *What to Do With the Kid Who . . . : Developing Cooperation, Self-Discipline, and Responsibility in the Classroom* (2nd ed.), *Designing Professional Portfolios for Change* and *How to Assess Authentic Learning* (4th ed.).

**CORWIN
PRESS**

The Corwin Press logo—a raven striding across an open book—represents the union of courage and learning. Corwin Press is committed to improving education for all learners by publishing books and other professional development resources for those serving the field of PreK–12 education. By providing practical, hands-on materials, Corwin Press continues to carry out the promise of its motto: **"Helping Educators Do Their Work Better."**

INTRODUCTION

Authenticity is the curriculum goal in which we help students acquire real-world skills and knowledge by developing their abilities to read, write, solve problems, and apply concepts in a manner that prepares them for their lives beyond school.

—Strong, Silver, and Perini (2001, p. 9)

Definition

Authentic learning focuses on what is real. The word authentic comes from the Greek word *autarkos*, meaning self-originating. Strong, Silver, and Perini (2001) describe how the word was transformed by Rousseau and later by Heidegger and Sartre into the emblem for the fullness of being. Authenticity to the philosophers meant a life lived without falsehoods, built upon a genuine and ever-expanding knowledge of the world and one's self. Strong, Silver, and Perini believe that "By placing a premium on authenticity in education, someone was obviously attempting to think differently about education, to consider fully the question of how school and life are interrelated" (p. 94). "Relevance" becomes an essential motivator for students of all ages. Students search for ways to connect their schoolwork to their own lives in order to find value in education beyond grades, credits, and standardized test scores.

Rationale

When students try to solve real-life problems, they see the relevance of schoolwork and are more likely to transfer the content and skills they learn in class by applying them to real problems or challenges. When students write letters to city council members supporting a ban on smoking in public places, they have not only a purpose for writing but also a purpose for using letter-writing skills. When students organize an orientation program to welcome new students to their school, they integrate problem-solving skills, writing skills, technology skills, and interpersonal skills in order to complete an authentic project. They understand why one has to utilize a variety of interrelated skills from different subject areas to accomplish the task of welcoming new students to their school.

If schoolwork is authentic and relevant, students engage in their learning and become active participants in the class.

Research

Authentic learning with its rich open-ended projects, performances, portfolios, and problem-solving tasks necessitates the need to develop authentic assessments to measure progress towards meeting the goals. Traditional multiple-choice tests that include only restricted and extended response items are limited when it comes to assessing open-ended, subjective, or creative work. Assessment, moreover, differs from evaluation. Evaluation is viewed as the summative measure of how much content a student has retained. It is most often used for grouping students and for assigning final grades. Assessment, on the other hand, requires the ongoing gathering of information that provides valuable insight to the teacher about how to guide and re-adjust instruction to meet the needs of all students.

Costa and Kallick (2004a) believe assessment should be neither summative nor punitive. They believe instead that assessment is a mechanism for providing ongoing feedback to the learner and to the organization as a necessary part of the spiraling processes of continuous renewal: self-managing, self-monitoring, and self-modifying. They believe students need to take ownership of their learning. When teachers provide students with tools such as study questions, graphic organizers, checklists, and rubrics, the students become empowered to take the lead in self-assessing and self-modifying their work. As Costa and Kallick state:

> We must constantly remind ourselves that the ultimate purpose of evaluation is to have students learn to become self-evaluative. If students graduate from our schools still dependent upon others to tell them when they are adequate, good, or excellent, then we've missed the whole point of what self-directed learning is about. (p. 117)

Jerald (2001) did an analysis of high-flying schools where students succeeded despite socioeconomic differences. His analysis showed that schools that were successful despite disadvantages had seven characteristics in common. The majority of the characteristics deal with standards, assessment, and appropriate professional development. One characteristic discusses the importance of using state standards to not only design curriculum and instruction but also assess student work. Another key characteristic states the importance of using assessments to help guide instruction. Stiggins (2002) discusses how the evolution of assessment in the United States over the past 5 decades has evolved into a new belief system. The public's perception of assessment focuses on school improvement that includes higher achievement standards, rigorous assessments, and the expectation of accountability on the part of educators for student achievement, as reflected in test scores. He says that the public relies

STANDARDS-BASED TEACHING

1. Teachers embed the vocabulary (words, people, events, and concepts) from the standards into their curriculum, instruction, and assessment.

2. Teachers monitor students' progress towards meeting and exceeding the standards by the ongoing use of checklists and rubrics to examine student work.

Figure 0.1

on "high-stakes assessments *of learning* to inform our decisions about accountability. These tests tell us how much students have learned, whether standards are being met, and whether educators have done the job they were hired to do" (p. 759).

In addition to the assessments *of learning* that provide evidence of achievement for public reporting, educators need to focus on assessments *for learning* that serve to help students learn more. Classroom assessments correlated with curriculum goals and standards provide feedback on an ongoing basis to teachers and students. The continuous flow of information targeted at student achievement helps students improve. Teachers focus on adjusting instruction based on the results of the classroom assessments. They modify, adapt, and regroup as needed. Since formative assessments are ongoing, they provide continuous feedback about the students' strengths and weaknesses. The teacher uses observations and feedback to modify the content, process, and product and adjust the pace for all or some of the students, depending upon their needs.

Balanced Assessment

Classroom assessments come in many shapes and sizes, but most of them fit into three categories: traditional, portfolio, and performance. All three provide valuable data to assess the whole child. Traditional assessments such as quizzes, teacher-made tests, and standardized tests measure knowledge of content and skills. Portfolios focus on a student's products, process, and progress over time and help students self-assess their work as well as set new goals for themselves. Portfolios also allow students to express themselves utilizing a wide variety of multiple intelligences. Performance assessments show how the performance standards are implemented. They require students to apply their knowledge of the content and their skills in a real task. Because many of the performances, projects, and products are creative and subjective in nature, teachers need to assess them in different ways. A traditional multiple-choice test would not be suitable to evaluate an oral presentation or a letter to the editor. Therefore, checklists and rubrics provide the guidelines and the criteria for grading. No single form of assessment by itself is adequate to measure the whole child. If a teacher uses all three measurements in appropriate proportions for the grade level, however, a true portrait of the student as a learner emerges.

BALANCED ASSESSMENT MODEL

Type of Assessment	Focus	Features
Traditional	• Knowledge • Curriculum • Skills	Classroom Assessments • Tests • Quizzes • Assignments Standardized Tests • Norm-Referenced • Criterion-Referenced
Portfolio	• Process • Product • Growth	• Growth and Development • Reflection • Goal Setting • Self-Evaluation
Performance	• Standards • Application • Transfer	• Tasks • Checklists • Rubrics • Examination of Student Work

Figure 0.2

Adapted from Burke, K., Fogarty, R., & Belgrad, S. (2002). *The Portfolio Connection: Student Work Linked to Standards,* 2nd Ed., p. 6. Thousand Oaks, CA: Corwin Press. Used with permission.

Differentiation

In today's differentiated classroom, assessments provide diagnostic as well as continuous feedback. Tomlinson (1999) believes the goal of assessment is to provide teachers with day-to-day data on students' readiness for particular ideas and skills based upon their interests and their learning profiles. Assessment is essential to teaching. Classroom assessments and grading procedures constitute integral components of instruction. The relationship between instruction and assessment has been compared to the infinity sign where one cannot see where instruction ends and assessment begins. It is a continuous feedback loop. In fact, many people believe assessment drives instruction because teachers begin with the end in mind—achieving the standards—and then plan backwards and create the tasks the students will need to complete in order to achieve the targeted outcomes. Because most states now provide standards to all teachers, the amount of guesswork teachers use to determine what's really important compared to what's "nice to know" has been greatly reduced. Now all the stakeholders know the target and are working together toward meeting the same goal.

Assessment is the ongoing process of gathering information for the purpose of making sound decisions to guide the teacher's instruction. Teaching is conceptualized today as a process of effective decision making. "This includes deciding what to teach, how to teach it, how long to teach, whether to group students, what questions to ask, what follow-up questions to ask, what to review, when to review, and so forth" (McMillan, 2001; p. 3). Because each class and each student are different, it doesn't make sense for a school or district to mandate prescriptive lesson plans and timelines. Specific lesson plans provide needed guidelines, of course, but each teacher adjusts the timelines and requirements as needed. If the students master the standards early, why prolong the unit? By the same token, if all the students need more time, or if some of the students need more time, they should get it. "Staying on topic" or "meeting the deadline" should not take precedence over student understanding.

Assessment is more than a documentation of learning—it is learning. Teachers who integrate relevant and valid assessments on an ongoing basis with their teaching and who are willing to make necessary adjustments to facilitate student learning help their students not only achieve higher academic goals but also achieve more fulfilling personal goals.

Classroom Assessments

Even though the public and policymakers look to high-stakes standardized test results to measure learning, the classroom assessments created by teachers are truly the key to improving student learning. The quizzes, writing assignments, journals, performances, projects, and portfolios that teachers administer on a regular basis provide the data teachers use to monitor and adjust their teaching to help students each day. Guskey (2003) asserts that teachers "trust the results from these assessments because of their direct relation to classroom instructional goals. Plus, results are immediate and easy to analyze at the individual student level" (p. 7). Teachers need to realize the importance of their ongoing assessments because they are an integral part of the instructional process. Teachers who get immediate results can adjust, modify, or redirect their teaching to help the students before the final evaluations. Because formative assessments are ongoing, they provide the most valuable feedback both to the student and to the teacher. Because summative evaluations are final, it is too late to make any adjustments or to change strategies because they come at the end of the assessment cycle and represent the final judgment of the students' performance. McMillan (2001) discusses several of the purposes of classroom assessments. He believes classroom assessments should identify if students have mastered a concept or skill. They should, he states, also communicate their expectations to students as well as motivate them to learn and take more ownership in self-evaluating their own work. By thoughtfully using assessment data, the teacher can modify the content, process, or product. According to Tomlinson (1999):

- **Content** is what teachers want students to learn and the materials or mechanisms through which that is accomplished.

- **Process** describes activities designed to ensure that students use key skills to make sense out of essential ideas and information.

- **Products** are vehicles through which students demonstrate and extend what they have learned. (p. 11)

From *The Differentiated Classroom: Responding to the Needs of All Students,* C. A. Tomlinson (1999) Copyright (c) The Association for Supervision and Curriculum Development. Reprinted with permission. The Association for Supervision and Curriculum Development is a worldwide community of educators advocating sound policies and sharing best practices to achieve the success of each learner. To learn more, visit ASCD at www.ascd.org

Standardized Tests

Large-scale assessments are designed for a specific purpose. The tests used in most states today are designed to rank-order schools and students for the purposes of accountability. Guskey (2003), however, feels that "assessments designed for ranking are generally not good instruments for helping teachers improve their instruction or modify their approach to individual students" (p. 7).

The *No Child Left Behind Act* of 2001 mandates annual testing of students in grades three through eight in reading and mathematics, and recent proposals advocate yearly testing through high school. According to Amrein and Berliner (2003), the federal legislators who overwhelmingly passed this act into law apparently assumed that high-stakes tests would improve student motivation and raise student achievement. Because testing programs similar to those required by *No Child Left Behind* already exist in many states, Amrein and Berliner believe the results should be analyzed to see if the tests are effective. Eighteen states currently use exams to grant or withhold diplomas, and most of the states also attach to their state assessments a broad range of other consequences for students, teachers, and schools. Amrein and Berliner state:

> Unfortunately, the evidence shows that such tests actually decrease student motivation and increase the proportion of students who leave school early. Further, student achievement in the 18 high-stakes testing states has not improved on a range of measures, such as the National Assessment of Educational Progress (NAEP), despite higher scores on the states' own assessments. (p. 32)

States that design high-stakes tests to correlate with their state standards differ from the more traditional norm-referenced testing system, which was designed to be secret and normed to fit a bell curve. Meier (2002) believes the new kind of state test can be directly taught to, and does not require as much secrecy regarding content. It also no longer requires scores distributed along a predetermined curve. Meier states that the tests "are intended to show whether teachers and students are doing their prescribed jobs: teachers teaching to the tests and students learning what's on them. It's called curriculum and test alignment" (p. 192). Meier worries about the states scoring their own tests under the direction of political officials in state departments. She feels the officials have the power of "weighting" subsections and "thus the actual scores and what constitutes failure, what constitutes needs improvement, what constitutes proficient—are in many states not decided until after the results are in and state officials can estimate the impact of their decisions" (p. 192). She says that the meaning of a score on these new tests rests not with the neutral bell curve, but with judgments made by some politically appointed body—ideally in collaboration with educational experts.

Researchers report that when states attach rewards and sanctions to performance on tests, students became less intrinsically motivated to learn and less likely to engage in critical thinking. Sheldon and Biddle (1998, as cited in Amrein & Berliner, 2003) found that high-stake tests cause teachers to take greater control of the learning experiences of their students, thereby denying their students opportunities to direct their own learning and construct knowledge for themselves. When the stakes get high, teachers no longer "encourage students to explore the concepts and subjects that interest them. Attaching stakes to tests apparently obstructs students' paths to becoming lifelong, self-directed learners and alienates students from their own learning experiences in school" (pp. 32–33). Instead of using their natural curiosity to solve a problem that is relevant to them, students tend to become passive learners who listen to their teacher's instruction rather than become active learners who search for deeper understandings that impact their own lives. Sousa (1995) reviewed the research that describes how much students retain twenty-four hours later based upon the type of teaching. The lecture method alone fosters a 5% retention rate and is at the top of the pyramid; students who discuss retain 50%, students who perform a task retain 75%, and students who either teach others or use the information immediately retain 95% (see Figure 0.3). Thus, the image of a teacher lecturing and a student passively taking notes without interacting with the teacher, the class members, or the information foreshadows a marginal learning experience. It also foreshadows a student who remembers the information for Friday's test, but will probably forget the information when it is time to apply it in a real-life situation.

Sheldon and Biddle (1998) found that older students depict themselves as anxious, angry, and withdrawn from high-stakes tests; moreover, they are more disillusioned and hostile towards tests than are younger students. The younger students may not yet realize the importance of the tests to their academic futures, and they still value their love of learning without the fear or pressure of failing a test and being retained.

Standards-Aligned Assessments

Because of the increased emphasis on standardized testing, many teachers have totally abandoned or greatly reduced the time spent setting a relevant context for learning experiences. Teachers sometimes dismiss proven instructional strategies, such as interdisciplinary curriculum that is vibrant and relevant, because they feel such strategies are too time consuming or impossible to implement in the today's climate of high-stakes testing. Drake

TEACHING METHODS AND RETENTION RATE

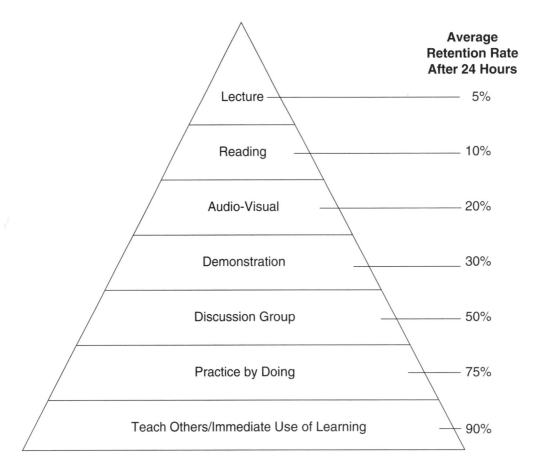

Figure 0.3

Sousa (1995). *How the Brain Learns*, 2nd Ed. Thousand Oaks, CA: Corwin Press. Reprinted with permission.

and Burns (2004) believe the advent of standards-based education, with its emphasis on disciplines, has largely displaced integrated curriculum, where students see the connections among subject areas and synthesize their learnings to solve problems. They fear that teachers have time to cover only "topics" such as "dinosaurs" or "Canada" without delving into the big concepts such as "extinction" and "interdependence" that lead to a deeper understanding of a topic. Although the search for connections, deeper meanings, and critical thinking does take more time, the students who achieve this in-depth understanding will be better equipped to transfer all the skills to other classes and life.

Specific content standards indicate what students must be able *to know* and *to do* at each grade level. In many cases, educators align these standards with evaluation procedures, both local assessments and standardized tests. Drake and Burns (2004) worry that the demands to cover the standards and help students perform well on standardized tests overwhelm teachers and students and take the joy out of teaching. They believe that when educators simply "cover" the standards, the students lack engagement because some of the lessons become dull and tedious for both teachers and students. When there are too many standards to address, teachers "cover" the information superficially and sometimes sacrifice quality for quantity. Instead of achieving deep understanding of key concepts, students focus on cursory coverage that concentrates on factual knowledge at the expense of enduring understanding.

Even though politicians and policymakers may expect all standards to be addressed equally, teachers need to prioritize the most important standards and integrate them into relevant tasks. Drake and Burns (2004) note that teachers "can chunk the standards together into meaningful clusters both within and across disciplines. Once teachers understand how standards are connected, their perception of interdisciplinary curriculum shifts dramatically. What they once saw as an impossible venture becomes an attractive alternative" (p. 2).

Classroom Assessments vs. Standardized Tests

In the balanced assessment model, teachers utilize traditional tests and standardized tests as well as classroom assessments to develop an accurate learning profile of each student. When used together, they both provide valuable data for the purpose of improving student achievement. It is evident that both standardized tests and classroom assessments used in conjunction with each other provide different types of data that present a more accurate profile of a student as a learner.

STANDARDIZED TESTS VS. CLASSROOM ASSESSMENTS

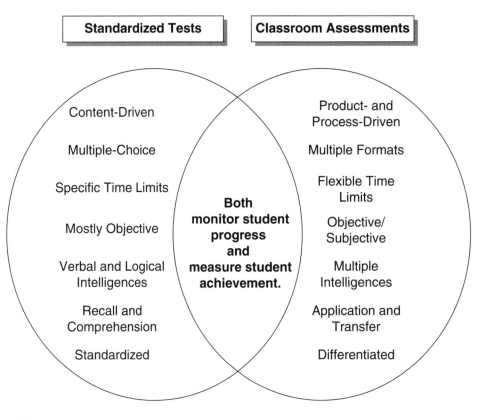

Standardized Tests	Classroom Assessments
Content-Driven	Product- and Process-Driven
Multiple-Choice	Multiple Formats
Specific Time Limits	Flexible Time Limits
Mostly Objective	Objective/Subjective
Verbal and Logical Intelligences	Multiple Intelligences
Recall and Comprehension	Application and Transfer
Standardized	Differentiated

Both monitor student progress and measure student achievement.

Figure 0.4

Burke, K. (2005) *How to Assess Authentic Learning,* 4th Ed. Thousand Oaks, CA: Corwin Press. Used with permission.

The Balanced Life

Philosophers Rousseau, Heidegger, and Sartre saw the value of the authentic life, lived without falsehoods and built upon a genuine and ever-expanding knowledge of the world and one's self. So, too, should educators place a premium on authenticity in education and focus on how to help students realize how school and life are interrelated. To achieve the balance in life and the balance in assessment, teachers need to integrate standardized tests and classroom assessments. They can accomplish this task by constructing meaningful and relevant learning experiences and assessments to target standards within the context of real-life problems that prepare students for the challenges of life.

The Six-Step Process

One way that teachers can target the standards and address real problems is to follow a six-step process when planning their curriculum units. The steps include targeting the important standards according to the data. Once teachers target the standards, they "unpack" them to find the "big ideas" and the "essential questions" that will help guide their instruction. Using the criteria embedded in state standards to create a teacher checklist will organize their teaching. Any assignment or assessment that integrates the key ideas of the standards will make the work more valid. Once the teachers target the standards, find the big ideas and essential questions, and organize their teaching, they are ready to design a meaningful and complex performance task that will motivate students to learn.

The final two steps involve helping the students understand the process for meeting a goal by giving them checklists to guide them through the steps of completing an assignment. Once the students acquire the information or skills they need in the checklist, they are ready to improve the quality of their work. The rubric provides the quality descriptors that tell students, "How good is good enough?" Students now know exactly what they have to accomplish to meet or exceed expectations for excellence.

The following six chapters review in more detail how to develop a process that moves the teachers and students from the standards to the rubrics in order to meet academic goals.

FROM STANDARDS TO RUBRICS IN SIX STEPS

Step 1:	**Target the Standards**	How can teachers work collaboratively to analyze data and target the standards?
Step 2:	**Find the Big Ideas**	How can teachers analyze the standards and determine the big ideas and essential questions that students will need to understand?
Step 3:	**Organize Teacher Checklists**	How can teachers define key terms from the standards and organize the criteria into checklists to guide their instruction?
Step 4:	**Create Performance Tasks**	How can teachers create motivating tasks correlated to curriculum and standards to establish a relevant context for the students?
Step 5:	**Develop Student Checklists**	How can teachers guide students sequentially through each step in the process of completing an assignment?
Step 6:	**Design Teaching Rubrics**	How good is good enough? How can students attain excellence by achieving the indicators described in the rubric?

Figure 0.5

CHAPTER 1

TARGET THE STANDARDS

Research repeatedly stresses the importance of collaboration within school environments and supports strong links between a sense of cooperative community and positive effect on schooling.

—Conzemius and O'Neill (2001, p. 67)

Definition

Targeting the standards is the process whereby teams of teachers analyze the data and work either as a team or learning community to design curriculum, implement appropriate instructional strategies, and develop assessments to meet the standards.

DuFour (2004) describes a professional learning community as a systematic process in which teachers work together to analyze and improve their classroom practice. He believes the professional learning community model focuses on the core mission of education—student learning. Rather than emphasizing what the teacher taught, the emphasis is instead on what the student learned. DuFour believes that every professional in the building must engage his or her colleagues in the ongoing exploration of three crucial questions that drive the work of those within a professional learning community:

(1) What do we want each student to learn?

(2) How will we know when each student has learned it?

(3) How will we respond when a student experiences difficulty in learning? (p. 8)

When teachers collaborate to learn the answers to these three critical questions, they engage in rich conversations that guide their instruction and their assessment. Teachers analyze the data and target the important standards that students need and then work collaboratively to design powerful curriculum units and authentic assessments to help all students succeed.

Rationale

The title of Ernest Hemingway's novel *For Whom the Bell Tolls* is from the theologian John Donne's 1623 sermon *Meditation 17*. Part of the sermon reads, "No man is an island entire of itself; every man is a piece of the continent, a part of the main . . . any man's death diminishes me, because I am involved in mankind, and therefore never send to know for whom the bell tolls; it tolls for thee" (Donne, 1623). Donne warned his parishioners to be concerned about their fellow man and to grieve for any man who dies—not just friends and relatives. Hemingway used the same theme when he wrote about the Spanish Civil War in the 1930s and warned how the world's apathy could signify bigger problems to come if people ignored the plight of their fellow man.

Failing students and failing schools may not be as life threatening or dramatic as war, peace, or death. There is, however, a parallel between the traditional isolation of the classroom teacher and high-stakes testing. It is not enough for classroom teachers to walk into the classroom, shut the door, and worry only about their students' development. It is important for all students in the school community to do well on their classroom assessments and on state and national assessments. In today's world of *No Child Left Behind* legislation and sanctions for "Needs Improvement Lists," teachers must abandon the island mentality in a school or district. Everyone must work together as a community of learners to ensure no child is left behind. If the special-needs student, the English-as-a-second-language learner, or the at-risk student with behavior problems fails the high-stakes test, the entire school could face sanctions. It is not appropriate to blame parents, other teachers, or the students themselves for damaging a school's reputation; it is more important to work together as a school community to help all teachers and all students succeed. No teacher or student is an island; every student's failure diminishes everyone.

In recent years, organizations engaged in professional development and school reform have started "bringing teachers together to do *collectively* what they generally do alone; that is, look at student work and think about students' performance in the classroom" (Little, Gearhart, Curry, & Kafka, 2003, p. 185). The purpose of these collaborative efforts is to foster teacher learning which, in turn, fosters student learning. A professional community provides a spirit of collaboration where teachers work with other teachers, special education teachers, support staff, curriculum specialists, and administrators to achieve a common goal. Conzemius and O'Neill (2001) believe that "People in collaborative environments feel appreciated, valued, and respected; the system brings out the best in them. There is a hard sense of mission and goals" (p. 67).

Research

New research is showing that strategic planning done by "planners" before the school year begins is less effective than planning done by teaching practitioners throughout the school year. Schmoker (2004) believes most productive thinking is "continuous and simultaneous with action—that is, with teaching—as practitioners collaboratively implement, assess, and adjust instruction as it happens. The most productive combinations of thought and action occur in team-based, short-term experimental cycles" (p. 427). Teachers who, through short-term trial and error, find ways to improve students' persuasive writing or use a Venn diagram to help them learn how to compare and contrast items should celebrate their successes. Schmoker believes that when teams of teachers work together to achieve these short-term wins in specific areas where the assessment data show students are struggling, the chances of attaining continuous improvement are greater.

Educators throughout the world engage in a wide variety of processes to help improve student achievement. Almost all the processes in today's age of accountability involve data. Data are more than just reams of paper stored in school cabinets. Data lead to self-analysis and effective innovations and strategies. Schmoker (2001) states, "A rapidly growing number of schools have made a momentous discovery: when teachers regularly and collaboratively review assessment data for the purpose of improving practice to reach measurable achievement goals, something magical happens" (p. 1).

TEAM RESULTS

In order for teachers working in teams to get results, they must:

1. Focus substantially—though not exclusively—on assessing standards.

2. Review simple, readily available achievement data to set a limited number of measurable achievement goals in the lowest-scoring subjects or courses and target specific standards where achievement is low within that course or subject area.

3. Work regularly and collectively to design, adapt, and assess instructional strategies targeted directly at specific standards of low student performance revealed by the assessment data (e.g., "measurement" in math; "voice" in writing; "sight reading" in music).

Figure 1.1

Schmoker, M., "UP and Away—Lifting Low Performance," *Journal of Staff Development*, Spring 2002, Vol 23, No. 2. Excerpted with permission of the National Staff Development Council, www.nsdc.org, 2005. All rights reserved.

In addition, Schmoker (2002) has found substantial evidence that desirable results are virtually inevitable when teachers work in teams to assess standards. The teams meet to review achievement data and set a limited number of measurable goals. He recommends teachers focus on one standard, such as "measurement" in math or "voice" in writing, to target specific skills. He says that teams should "work regularly and collectively to design, adapt, and assess instructional strategies targeted directly at specific standards of low performance revealed by the assessment data" (p. 11).

Roy (2004b) describes how staff developers during the early 1970s focused on content. She states they were more concerned with the good presenters and good programs. The staff developers believed everything would fall into place provided the right content was selected. However, the Rand Studies published in 1978 found that many factors other than the content impacted the effectiveness or sustainability of the Title IV-C 3-year projects. The study showed that teacher involvement was necessary for project success and that even though district support was essential, neither top-down nor grass-root efforts were sufficient—collaboration was key. The study also described how the greater the scope of change, the more time and effort were required. The study authors also recommended that the "staff may need to 'reinvent' their own process for implementation—implementation plans cannot be *taken off the shelf*" (Roy, 2004b, p. 3).

In other words, the *process* was as important as the *content,* and few formal programs developed by others meet all the needs of the district. Roy (2004b) describes process as the use of data to determine priority goals, the development of collegiality to support change, the use of a variety of models and designs to ensure development of knowledge and skills, and the quality implementation of innovations. As a result of research, classroom coaching is now considered a *necessity,* not a frill, if quality implementation is to occur. Even top performers in sports or in the classroom never outgrow their need for coaching. What worked in the past or what worked for most students may not work today with students.

Guastello (2004) believes that parents should also be included in the community of learners because they are the key motivating dynamic in a child's life. Parents must also understand the expectations placed on their child in terms of learning outcomes and achievement. She cites Walberg's 1984 research that contends "parent involvement and home factors are more important for student achievement than are student characteristics, instructional strategies, environmental factors, and increased time in academic learning" (p. 80). Teachers can help students know the expectations for quality work; parents can reinforce and support the teachers' efforts by helping the students at home.

Roy (2004b, p. 3) discusses the importance of the Results-Based Process that involves both teacher and student learning. The process begins with three steps:

(1) Determine what students need to know and be able to do.

(2) Determine what teachers need to know and be able to do.

(3) Plan and design staff development to accomplish the intended results.

By beginning with the end in mind, teachers plan backwards and design the performance task scenario, the activities, strategies, checklists, and rubrics that show evidence that the students have, in fact, mastered the standard. Hopefully, they will also attain a deep understanding of the important concepts embedded in the benchmarks and standards.

RESULTS-BASED PROCESS

What students need to know and be able to do.	What educators need to know and be able to do to ensure student success.	Professional development that ensures educators acquire necessary knowledge and skills.

Figure 1.2

Roy, Pat. "The Three Elements of the Standards," *Results,* November 2004. Excerpted with permission of the National Staff Development Council, www.nsdc.org, 2005. All rights reserved.

The Six-Step Process

The first step in the process described in this book involves bringing together teams of teachers to analyze both the formal data from test scores and the informal data from diagnostic and classroom assessments. The teachers then determine what key standards need to be addressed to help their students succeed. These grade-level or content-specific groups of teachers collaborate to design and implement the curriculum unit, select appropriate instructional strategies, and develop the authentic assessments they will use to help all the students in their classes. Once they decide what they need to do, the teachers may request a specific type of professional development that will help them achieve their own goals. In many schools, these teams engage in mini-action research projects to explore effective practices to help their students. Teachers become "embedded" staff developers who then coach or train other teachers to use the best practices.

Once they have analyzed the data, teachers examine the standards and generate the big ideas and the essential questions they want students to be able to understand and answer at the end of the unit. After "unpacking" the standards to find the key understanding, teachers break down the criteria in the standard and rearrange them in sequential order. When the key steps are arranged in sequential order, the teachers can more easily organize their own teaching. Teachers also focus on the vocabulary terms from the standards. After the teachers feel comfortable with the vocabulary terms and concepts, they design an engaging problem scenario. The performance task scenario should be linked directly to one of their curriculum units and designed to cluster many of the standards to provide a context. Students should be able to see why they must *use* all the content knowledge and skills they are learning. The tasks also motivate the students because they resemble real-life problems people regularly face in life.

The last two steps involve embedding all the vocabulary and essential ideas from the curriculum objectives and the standards into student-friendly checklists. The checklists provide the students with a step-by-step process to complete each of the projects and the performance. They also help teachers know which students still need help—before the project is due. Checklists also help students organize themselves so eventually they can accomplish the same task without the scaffolding provided by the teacher.

The final step addresses the issue of quality. Although the checklist tells the student what to include, it does not describe the levels of quality. When the criteria checklist is converted to an analytical rubric, it describes the degrees of quality and answers the age-old question, "How good is good enough?"

The final goal is to have teams of teachers collaborate once again to examine student work and provide consistent and specific feedback. The feedback guides their instruction and helps refocus students who still require help. The collaborative process can be adjusted to meet the needs of individual teachers and students.

FROM STANDARDS
TO RUBRICS IN SIX STEPS

Step 1:	**Target the Standards**	How can teachers work collaboratively to analyze data and target the standards?
Step 2:	**Find the Big Ideas**	How can teachers analyze the standard and determine the big ideas and the essential questions that students will need to understand?
Step 3:	**Organize Teacher Checklists**	How can teachers define key terms from the standards and organize the criteria into checklists to guide their instruction?
Step 4:	**Create Performance Tasks**	How can teachers create motivating tasks correlated to curriculum and standards to establish a relevant context for the students?
Step 5:	**Develop Student Checklists**	How can teachers guide students sequentially through each step in the process of completing an assignment?
Step 6:	**Design Teaching Rubrics**	How good is good enough? How can students attain excellence by achieving the indicators described in the rubric?

Figure 1.3

STEP 1: ANALYZE THE DATA AND TARGET THE STANDARDS

What are your data sources?

Based on the results of the third-grade state tests last year, students are having a difficult time writing a narrative in class and on standardized tests. The fourth-grade teachers agree that students do not understand the narrative writing process when they write papers in class. They tend to switch from a narrative approach to an expository approach in the middle of their papers and cannot maintain a consistent first-person point of view.

What areas of weakness need to be addressed?

We need to help students develop plot, establish point of view, include descriptive language, and organize a narrative appropriately.

What key standard targets this area of weakness?

Standard: The student demonstrates competence in a variety of genres. The student produces a narrative that:

a. engages the reader by establishing a context, creating a point of view, and otherwise developing reader interest;

b. establishes a plot, setting, conflict, and/or significance of events;

c. creates an organizing structure;

d. includes sensory details and concrete language to develop plot and character;

e. excludes extraneous details and inconsistencies;

f. develops complex characters through actions describing the motivation of characters and character conversation;

g. uses a range of appropriate narrative strategies such as dialogue, tension, or suspense;

h. provides a sense of closure to the writing.

Figure 1.4

APPLICATION

Step 1: Analyze the Data and Target the Standards

What are your data sources?

What areas of weakness need to be addressed?

What key standard targets this area of weakness?

Standard: _____

_____

_____

What are the criteria, indicators, or elements that describe this standard in detail?
List them.

Figure 1.5

TARGET THE STANDARDS

Reflection

Step 1:   Target the Standard   How can teachers work collaboratively to analyze data and target the standards?

1. What role do you think data plays in education today?

2. How do teachers in your school collaborate? Can you think of ways they could work together more often? Explain.

3. Reflect on how Standards-Based Teaching is impacting the way you teach.

Figure 1.6

CHAPTER 2

FIND THE BIG
IDEAS

*The students we interviewed equated good teaching
and learning with teachers that connected their subject
matter with real life experiences that students perceived
as interesting, relevant, meaningful and useful.
According to these students, effective learning that
achieves high standards is intimately related to the
integration of the school curriculum with the life
experiences of the students.*

—Storz and Nestor (2003, p. 17)

Definition

"Big Ideas" have been described as the key concepts or enduring understandings that have challenged mankind from the beginning of time. They transcend topics and subject areas and cities and states because they focus on universal themes and try to answer provocative questions such as, "Why does man create?"

Teachers new to the profession might not remember the era of behavioral objectives and mastery learning. Many people see a parallel with standards and worry about how to cover them all before students take the high-stakes tests that are now required to pass each grade at the elementary levels and graduate from most high schools. Veteran teachers remember the five-inch binders filled with curriculum goals and behavioral objectives that were almost impossible to cover in one school year. Art Costa, Emeritus Professor of Education at California State University, Sacramento, a noted educator and others recommended that teachers might need to "selectively abandon" some of their hundreds of objectives in order to focus on the things that were most important. Unfortunately, many teachers found it difficult to prioritize their curriculum on their own and focus on the key foundation pieces that students would need to be successful in their courses.

Standards, conversely, tend to be more focused. They synthesize the body of knowledge that a group of educators agrees is necessary for success in each subject area and at each grade level. Even though administrators, teachers, parents, and students feel the pressure of meeting the standards and achieving on the high-stakes standardized tests, most people know that learning involves more than passing one or two tests. Unfortunately, some teachers feel the accountability pressure and abandon their engaging units that challenge their students to "think outside the box" in order to be able to "check off" that they "covered" the standard.

In the process of "covering the curriculum and the standards," it is possible to lose sight of the importance of why students study certain things and what are the key concepts that are universal enough to transfer into other subject areas and into life itself. Students may study the Civil War in social studies class, but the key concept of "conflict" transcends the 1860s and can be studied in every war as well as literature, politics, social issues, and, perhaps most important, their own lives. The big ideas focus on the enduring understandings and the key concepts that transfer into every aspect of learning. The essential questions guide students to a deeper understanding of human values, ambitions, and driving forces as the students strive to find the answers to questions they have about their world and, most important, themselves.

Rationale

The content students learn often becomes obsolete in today's technology-driven world; therefore, it is important for teachers to help students understand the meaning of life. The universal themes of literature, for example, describe the literature of the ancient Greeks as well as the contemporary literature of the twenty-first century. Why does man create? How does power corrupt? Why do we go to war? These questions cannot be answered on a multiple-choice Scantron test. There is just too much information to learn. When teachers analyze or "unpack" the standards to uncover the key ideas within the content, they help students see the big ideas rather than just the isolated facts.

Research

McTighe and Thomas (2003) worry that reducing desired learning to only those items that are measurable on a large-scale assessment results in an "unhealthy narrowing of the curriculum and decontextualized multiple-choice teaching methods" (p. 52). They also believe that teachers should not be focusing solely on covering the decontextualized standards. Instead, the primary goals of teaching and learning should be "understanding key concepts and searching for answers to provocative questions—essential questions that human beings perennially ask about the world and themselves" (p. 52). Therefore, the primary focus of any school improvement initiative should be the understanding of the key ideas embedded in the content standards. If students seek answers to important questions, they will "learn important facts, concepts, and skills—those that typically appear on standardized tests—in the context of exploring and applying larger ideas" (p. 52).

The term most often used to describe this process is called "unpacking" the standard. By breaking down the standard, teachers uncover the key ideas within the content in order to develop essential questions. The big ideas and essential questions provide a conceptual lens through which teachers address the content. An example of "unpacking the standard" given by McTighe and Thomas (2003) involves a 7th Grade State History Standard: *"Compare the early civilizations of the Indus River Valley with those of China's Yellow River Region."*

An unpacked version might examine the following big ideas and companion essential questions:

- The geography, climate, and natural resources of a region influence how its inhabitants live and work. How does where people live influence how they live?
- Cultures share common features while retaining distinctive qualities. What makes a culture? Are modern civilizations more civilized than ancient ones?
- The past offers insights into historical patterns, universal themes, and recurring aspects of the human condition. What can we learn from studying other places and times?" (McTighe & Thomas, 2003, p. 53)

From McTighe & Thomas, Backward Design for Forward Action, *Educational Leadership, 60*(5), p. 53. (C) 2003, The Association for Supervision and Curriculum Development. Reprinted with permission. The ASCD is a worldwide community of educators advocating sound policies and sharing best practices to achieve the success of each learner. To learn more, visit ASCD at www.ascd.org

Drake and Burns (2004) believe teachers meet standards through using an integrated approach to studying the curriculum. They believe that students who study traditional topics that are limited do not see the big ideas unless teachers help them understand the higher-level concept. Because concepts are more universal than topics, they can be applied in many subject areas and throughout life. Understanding concepts also requires students to use higher-level thinking skills, skills that stretch them to, e.g., compare and contrast civilizations; analyze why men start wars; synthesize the research on conservation; determine the causes of a recession and the effects it has on the markets, jobs, and people's lives; and evaluate the importance of identity for a country, race, sex, or individual. Drake and Burns (see Figure 2.1) believe teachers should start with a topic of study and then expand the topic into a concept that includes big ideas and essential questions that may or may not be answered while studying the topic. These provocative questions challenge students to think and help them understand that not all questions have answers.

ADDING A CONCEPTUAL
FOCUS TO A TOPIC

Topic	Possible Conceptual Focus/Theme
Dinosaurs	Extinction
Canada	Interdependence
Medieval Times	Culture
Consumerism	Cause and Effect
Community	Identity
Evolution	Diversity
Butterflies	Cause and Effect
Civil War	Conflict
	Drake & Burns, 2004, p. 43

Figure 2.1

Drake, S. M., & Burns, R. C. (2004). *Meeting Standards Through Integrating Curriculum.* Alexandria, VA: Association for Supervision and Curriculum Development. Reprinted with permission. The Association for Supervision and Curriculum Development is a worldwide community for educators advocating sound policies and sharing best practices to achieve the success of each learner. To learn more, visit ASCD at www.ascd.org.

Figure 2.2 shows how to target a writing standard that requires students to demonstrate competency in the writing process. The standard is broken down into what students need to know (declarative knowledge—content) and what they need to be able to do (procedural knowledge—performance). Teachers then meet as a team and write two columns about what the teachers need to know (declarative knowledge—content) and what the teachers need to be able to do (procedural knowledge—performance) before they teach the standard to their students. If teachers feel comfortable with the vocabulary words, content, and process, they will be better prepared to teach others.

When teachers work collaboratively to "unpack" the standard, the process helps each teacher know exactly what is involved in teaching the targeted standard. Roy (2004a) and others believe that if teachers do not feel prepared to teach the writing process, they should request the professional development they need. They can get help either informally, from peers on their collaborative planning

WHAT STUDENTS SHOULD
KNOW AND BE ABLE TO DO

The Writing Process	
What students should know/understand: *(Declarative Knowledge)*	**What students should be able to do:** *(Procedural Knowledge)*
Key Facts:	**Skills:**
• Story hooks to motivate readers	• Students practice writing motivating hooks to grab their audience's attention
• Point-of-view (1st person, 3rd person, etc.) used to tell a narrative	• Students analyze a piece of writing and define the point of view of the story. They then write a story from a specific point of view (1st person, 3rd person)
• Writing patterns (chronological, cause and effect)	• Students analyze pieces of writing to determine the specific patterns (chronological order, cause and effect) the authors use to tell their stories. They then write their own story using a specific writing pattern.

• Writing Process
  – Brainstorm
  – Outline
  – Revise
  – Edit
  – Share with peer
	• Students write a narrative using:
	  – Brainstorming
	  – Outlining
	  – Revising
	  – Editing
	  – Peer sharing

Figure 2.2

teams, or formally, during professional workshops or courses. If teachers do not feel that they are proficient in the elements of the standards, they will not feel confident, and they probably will not be as effective when it comes to teaching the standard to the students. When teachers collaborate in small groups, they feel more comfortable asking their peers to explain the key components of the standard and to provide strategies to help them teach the standard to the students. Roy contends that building staff development content on this foundation means the content is not based on "hot topics" and "silver bullets," but rather grounded in the needs of students and their teachers (p. 3).

Fifth-Grade Social Studies Standards

Another example of unpacking a standard involves a fifth-grade social studies standard. Teachers can review the fifth-grade social studies standard that states: The student will (1) analyze and explain major causes and effects of World War II, (2) analyze and explain major events of World War II, and (3) analyze and explain World War II personalities.

After the teachers work together to analyze the standard and all its descriptors, indicators, benchmarks, and elements, they may decide on the following:

- Big Idea

   People in power may influence major world events.

- Essential Questions

   How did specific events cause World War II?

   Why do countries decide to start or enter a war?

   How do personalities of people influence the course of a war?

   What are some of the major effects of World War II?

Created by members of the North Springs Assessment Cluster. Used with permission of the Fulton County Board of Education, Georgia.

If teachers work in team to analyze the standards, they work collaboratively to develop the big idea that the students should understand by the end of the unit. Teachers then write meaningful and thoughtful essential questions that will guide their students through the process of looking at the concepts, themes, or patterns that focus on the compelling questions. By answering these essential questions, students arrive at a better understanding of the topic, the world they live in, and, most important, themselves.

The Process

The Performance Task Unit Cover Sheet (Figure 2.6) at the end of this chapter provides a guide to record information related to the standard and the process

BIG IDEAS AND
ESSENTIAL QUESTIONS

Content	Big Ideas and Essential Questions
First-Grade Social Studies **Standard:** The student will read about and describe the life of historical figures in American history.	**Big Idea:** The contributions of historical figures impact history. **Essential Questions:** Why could George Washington Carver be called a nutty professor? How is Benjamin Franklin "electrifying"? Why was Harriet Tubman's "railroad" a secret?
Fourth/Fifth-Grade Math **Standard:** The student will explore the concept of mean and median and collect, read, interpret, and compare data from charts, tables, and graphs using a variety of scales and estimates.	**Big Idea:** Charts, tables, and graphs present data in visual ways that makes it easier to understand the math concept. **Essential Questions:** Why do we need to know the difference between mean and median? How do charts, tables, and graphs display data so that people can understand math better?

Figure 2.3

Created by members of the Tri-Cities/Banneker Assessment Cluster. Used with permission of Fulton County Board of Education, Georgia.

that takes a teacher from Step One, Analyzing the Standard, to Step Two, Determining Big Ideas and Essential Questions.

The following chapters address the next four steps of developing teacher checklists, performance tasks, student checklists, and rubrics—all correlated to curriculum goals and state standards. The journey begins with the end in mind. Standards are the alpha and the omega—the beginning and the end—of the journey.

APPLICATION—ANALYZE THE STANDARD

Step 1: After reviewing the data, select a standard that you want to target for your students. After carefully analyzing the standard, benchmarks, indicators, and elements, list what both students and teachers need to know and be able to do in order to address the standard.

Standard: _____

_____

_____

What <u>students</u> should be able to do: *(Declarative Knowledge/Content)* **Key Facts:**	What <u>students</u> should know/understand: *(Procedural Knowledge/Performance)* **Skills:**
What <u>teachers</u> should be able to do: *(Declarative Knowledge/Content)* **Key Facts:**	What <u>teachers</u> should know/understand: *(Procedural Knowledge/Performance)* **Skills:**

Figure 2.4

APPLICATION—FIND BIG IDEAS AND DEVELOP ESSENTIAL QUESTIONS

Select a standard/benchmark that you want to address.

What are some big ideas or key concepts that students should explore within the context of the content and the standards?

What are <u>five</u> essential questions that students should be able to answer about the content and big ideas at the end of the unit?

1.

2.

3.

4.

5.

Figure 2.5

PERFORMANCE TASK
UNIT COVER SHEET

Teacher: _____ Subject(s): _____

Grade: _____

Curriculum Unit: _____

Time Frame for Unit: _____

Primary State Standards: Key standards all students have the opportunity to meet. (Individual Work and Assessments)

Secondary State Standards: Standards that some students have the opportunity to meet. (Group Work)

Big Ideas of Unit: List the key concepts, enduring understandings, principles, issues, or problems addressed in this unit.

Essential Questions: List three essential questions that guide your teaching and motivate students to uncover the important ideas at the heart of this subject area.

1.

2.

3.

Figure 2.6

FIND THE BIG IDEAS

Reflection

Step 2: Find the Big Ideas How can teachers analyze the standards and determine the big ideas and essential questions that students will need to understand?

1. Why do you feel it is important to focus on the big ideas before teaching a curriculum unit?

2. How can essential questions guide your instruction and focus the students?

Figure 2.7

CHAPTER 3

ORGANIZE TEACHER CHECKLISTS

In a standards-based system, grading and reporting must be criterion-referenced. Teachers at all levels must identify what they want their students to learn and be able to do and what evidence they will use to judge that achievement or performance. Grades based on clearly stated learning criteria have direct meaning and communicate that meaning.

—Guskey (2001, pp. 20–21)

Definition

Teacher checklists resemble lesson plans because they show each step teachers must cover as they introduce those steps developmentally to the students. Checklists contain the specific criteria, indicators, elements, or benchmarks that are embedded in the standards.

Criteria form the heart and soul of evaluation. Without clear criteria, judging a performance is subjective and somewhat arbitrary. Before standards, teachers who developed checklists created their own criteria to guide their instruction. Often the criteria would be derived from past experiences. For example, if a teacher had taught the skill of writing letters to the editor, she would know that in order for the letter to be effective students would have to include the following: *facts, statistics, quotes, persuasive arguments, topic sentences, support sentences, concluding sentences, and letter format such as date, salutation, inside address, body, and closing signature.* Many of these criteria are still applicable, but now the teacher also has to check the state standards in order to review the criteria listed to make sure the assessment will be valid when students take the state tests. The state standard may list other criteria, such as *point of view, voice, audience, focus, logical arguments, tone, and call to action.* If teachers use only their own criteria or the criteria in their textbooks, the students may do well on their classroom assessments, but they may get confused when they take the high-stakes state standardized tests if the terms are different. Often, teachers and principals analyze the data from state tests in order to find out which questions the students missed. They sometimes find that the students may have in fact learned the information, but they became confused because the vocabulary words used on the test were not the same vocabulary words used in their textbook or classwork. Figure 3.1 shows how different vocabulary words can confuse students on state tests.

The specific vocabulary of the standards can be very important if it involves a whole section like the writing test does. One state test asked the students to take a certain "focus statement" and develop it into a five-paragraph essay. Some of the students,who had practiced developing "thesis statements" into five-paragraph essays all year, did not understand what they were being asked to do. Their teachers were upset when the students told them that they had either not attempted the essay or had written something totally unrelated to

VOCABULARY WORDS

Teacher/Textbook	State Test
Types of Literature	Genre
Circle Graph	Pie Graph
Thesis Statement	Focus Statement
Main Character	Protagonist
Base Word	Root Word
Rename	Regroup
Verb	Predicate
Compare/Contrast	Similarities/Differences
Closure	Clincher
Noun	Naming Parts
Time-Order Words	Transitions

Figure 3.1

the task. Needless to say, a small vocabulary misunderstanding could cause students to repeat the fourth grade.

Teacher checklists list the sequential steps teachers need to take to teach the skills, and they also embed vocabulary words derived directly from the state standards. When criteria are "chunked," or "clustered," teachers understand how tasks are analyzed. Basically, a checklist is a mini-item analysis process where the teacher "deconstructs" or "dissects" the abstract standard, classifies big categories, and sequences the rest of the discrete skills into manageable steps. If teachers limit the categories to three or four classifications, they practice brain-compatible strategies that describe how the brain works best when multiple ideas are clustered into manageable chunks.

Criteria are most often used in assessments that judge subjective assignments such as essays, portfolios, products, or performances. When one refers to an assignment being criterion-referenced, it means that it is an approach for "describing a student's performance according to established criteria (e.g., she types 55 words per minute without errors)" (Arter & McTighe, 2001, p. 180). Criteria are the heart and soul of assessment because they specify qualities of excellence so that all the stakeholders know the target goals.

Rationale

Once teams of teachers have "unpacked" the standards and listed all the declarative knowledge and procedural knowledge both the teachers and students need to know, they organize the criteria into manageable chunks and then sequence them into the order in which they plan to teach them. Unfortunately, most state standards list all the benchmarks, descriptors, indicators, or elements (once again, vocabulary distinctions that cause confusion), but they are not necessarily listed in any kind of order. A writing standard might begin with the obvious, "Engage the reader" and it may end with the obvious "Bring closure to the piece," but everything in between is usually a random potpourri of unorganized descriptors. One process that many teachers use is the "sticky note" strategy. The teachers review the standard and then write each criterion on a separate small sticky note. They then step back and look at all the separate notes to see if they see some categories or classifications emerging. Once they see some big categories, like "Research," they use a bigger sticky note and label it "Research" and then move the sticky notes, such as "Internet sources," "books," "periodicals," "primary sources," and "secondary sources," under the bigger sticky note holding category. Sometimes all the essential criteria are included in the standard or benchmark, but other times, teachers have to add criteria they know that they will have to teach in order to help students understand the key ideas of the assignment. They might also have to reorganize the order of the steps because they know the logical progression of completing the task.

Teachers then make a vocabulary list of key terms that students will need to know in order to fully understand the standard. The vocabulary list includes nouns and verbs in the standard, key people or events, and definitions of thinking skills needed to understand the big ideas. This list could be taken from the State Standards Glossary or it could be developed from the definitions in the textbooks. It will also be important, however, to list several words as synonyms on the checklist to make sure that students will recognize words from their textbook and from the standards. For example, list "main character and protagonist;" "lead, motivator, and hook;" "circle graph and pie graph;" and "thesis statement," "main idea," and "focus statement" just to make sure students know that the terms mean basically the same thing.

Research

Guskey (2001) describes how teachers differentiate the types of criteria they use into three categories: product, process, and progress. The product criteria relate to students' specific achievement or levels of performance. They describe what students know and are able to do at that particular point in time. Guskey also discusses how teachers using product criteria base students' grades on final products such as projects, performances, reports, or portfolios as culminating demonstrations of learning. He also states that advocates of standards favor product criteria because it shows objectively whether or not a student meets the standards, regardless of process or effort. It provides a truer picture of competency and eliminates problems with grade inflation that sometimes accompany grading for process or progress. Basically, the grade is based solely on the final product and whether or not that product meets the criteria for quality work. Using product criteria to assess student work is closely aligned to the traditional assessment method used in schools today.

Process criteria relate not to the final results, but to how the students arrived at their final product. Guskey (2001) states that educators who believe that product criteria do not provide a complete picture of student learning generally favor process criteria because they consider "student effort, class behavior, or work habits [as well as] daily work, regular classroom quizzes, homework, class participation, punctuality of assignments, or attendance in determining students' grades" (pp. 21–22). The process criteria are important to teachers who want to penalize high-ability students who receive high grades with little effort as well as acknowledge the hard work of less talented students who must work diligently even to achieve low grades. If teachers consider only product criteria, however, some low-ability students who exert effort will be penalized and perhaps become disinterested in working. Moreover, they could perceive they are being treated unfairly and quit trying altogether.

Progress criteria relate to how much students actually gain from their learning experiences. Other terms teachers use include "learning gain," "value-added grading," "educational growth," and "improvement grading." Progress criteria emphasize how far a student has come rather than where he or she is now. For example, a struggling ESOL student may not meet the writing criteria for a standardized writing sample, but she may have moved from 20% mastery to 50% mastery or from a "0" to a "2" on a rubric. The grade would reflect the student's "learning potential" and would be individualized for each student.

When teachers combine the product, process, and progress criteria into a single grade in an attempt to be fair, it often results in an unclear grade that is difficult for students, parents, and administrators to interpret. When a parent sees an "A" on a report card, it is difficult to interpret. Guskey (2001) uses the example that an A "may mean that the student knew what the teacher expected before instruction began (product), didn't learn as well as expected but tried very hard (process), or simply made significant improvement (progress)" (p. 22).

The main focus of a teacher checklist is usually "products." Because the purpose of the standard is to show what something needs to look like if it is to be judged as meeting the standard, teachers need to prepare their standards-based teacher checklist with steps to achieve a final product. In chapter five, the focus is on student checklists that guide students in completing a final product. It would be appropriate to add criteria dealing with both process and progress at that time in order to honor student efforts and their own growth. That way, students and parents can see not only how well the student has met the standard, but also the process followed and the progress made towards meeting the standard.

Creating a Teacher Checklist

A teacher checklist may look easy, but it requires brainstorming, classification, prioritizing, and sequencing skills. In order for a checklist to be valid, it must also correlate to the vocabulary of the standards. The following steps are necessary.

TEAM APPROACH

Creating a standards-based teacher checklist helps guide each teacher through the steps necessary to teach the standards. Using the actual vocabulary from the standards, benchmarks, and indicators also makes the checklist more valid. Teams of teachers working together in a cooperative community environment discuss the most logical sequence for teaching the standard. It is interesting to

(Text continues on p.51)

CREATING A TEACHER CHECKLIST

Step One: Select a target standard and review the benchmarks, elements, or indicators listed under the standard.

Step Two: Write each of the criteria separately in the order they are mentioned and create a vocabulary list of nouns and verbs.

Step Three: Classify the criteria into categories that fit together by using main topics and subtopics.

Step Four: Fill in other criteria that might be needed to explain the process more clearly or to define abstract terms.

Step Five: Sequence the criteria in the order the skills will be taught.

Figure 3.2

GEORGIA NARRATIVE WRITING STANDARD—FOURTH GRADE

Step One: Review the Standard

Georgia English Language Arts, Fourth-Grade Writing Standard (ELA4W2)

ELA4W2: The student demonstrates competence in a variety of genres.
The student produces a narrative that:

    a. Engages the reader by establishing a context, creating a point of view, and otherwise developing reader interest.

    b. Establishes a plot, setting, and conflict, and/or the significance of events.

    c. Creates an organizing structure.

    d. Includes sensory details and concrete language to develop plot and character.

    e. Excludes extraneous details and inconsistencies.

    f. Develops complex characters through actions describing the motivation of characters and character conversation.

    g. Uses a range of appropriate narrative strategies such as dialogue, tension, or suspense.

    h. Provides a sense of closure to the writing.

Step Two: List each of the criteria separately in the order that is mentioned and create a vocabulary list of terms (including the verbs).

- Engages the reader
- Establishes a context
- Creates a point of view
- Develops reader interest
- Establishes a plot
- Establishes a setting
- Establishes a conflict
- Establishes the significance of events
- Creates an organizing structure
- Includes sensory details to develop plot and character
- Includes concrete language to develop plot and character

- Excludes extraneous details
- Excludes inconsistencies
- Develops complex characters
- Describes the motivation of characters
- Develops character conversation
- Uses narrative strategies such as dialogue
- Uses tension
- Uses suspense
- Provides a sense of closure to the writing

Step Three: Classify the criteria into categories that fit together. Add some more details to help students understand the terms used. The italicized phrases were added by the teachers.

Engages the Reader
- Establishes a Context
- Creates a Point of View
- Develops Reader Interest

Establishes a Story
- Develops a Plot
- Develops a Setting
- Develops a Conflict
- Develops the Significance of Events

Creates an Organizing Structure

- *Chronological Order*
- *Cause and Effect*
- *Similarities/Differences*
- *Posing and Answering a Question*

Includes Sensory Details

- *Uses Colorful Adjectives*
- *Uses Vivid Adverbs*
- *Uses Figurative Language*

Includes Concrete Details

- *Uses Action Verbs*
- *Uses Appropriate Nouns and Pronouns*

Excludes Extraneous Details

- *Eliminates Unnecessary Details*
- *Focuses on One Story Line*
- *Does not "Birdwalk"*

Excludes Inconsistencies

- *Checks for Continuity*
- *Checks for Coherency*
- *Checks Facts, Names, Plot Lines*

Develops Complex Characters

- *Portrays Realistic Protagonist*
- *Portrays Realistic Antagonist*
- *Uses Authentic Dialogue*

Uses Appropriate Narrative Strategies

- *Uses Dialogue to Drive Plot*
- *Establishes Tension for Plot*
- *Interjects Suspense Elements*

Provides a Sense of Closure to the Writing

- *Foreshadows the Ending*
- *Builds Story to Climax*
- *Develop Unraveling of Plot*
- *Answers Key Questions*
- *Wraps Up Loose Ends*

Step Four: Fill in any other criteria or steps that are needed to explain the process more clearly. Teachers need to add more details to help students understand what to do.

For Example:

"Creates an Organizing Structure" may seem a little vague to fourth-grade students, so the teacher can fill in specifics.

Creates an Organizing Structure

- Chronological Order
- Cause and Effect
- Similarities and Differences
- Posing and Answering a Question

"Includes Sensory Details" is another phrase that does not specify what fourth-graders can provide to enhance their writing. Therefore, teachers can give some suggestions students might consider to include in their narrative.

Includes Sensory Details
- Sight
- Touch
- Smell
- Sound

Sometimes the criteria may be clear, but teachers can still add a few hints to make sure students don't forget anything while they are writing their narrative. Leave a blank line so students fill in the answers. The checklist also serves as a study worksheet.

Establishes a Story
- Develops Plot (write in answer)
  - Who _____
  - What _____
  - Where _____
  - When _____
  - Why _____
  - How _____

- Develops Setting
  - Where _____
  - When _____

- Develops Conflict
  - Man vs. Man _____
  - Man vs. Nature _____
  - Man vs. Himself _____
  - Other _____

Step Five: Sequence the criteria in the order the skills will be taught.

Most state standards do not list the criteria embedded in the standards in a logical or sequential order. Teachers need to rearrange the criteria so they make sense—at least until students internalize the steps so they can complete any process automatically. Transfer doesn't take place until students can complete the performance without the "scaffolding" of the checklist for support. A veteran teacher who has taught the narrative multiple times knows the order that works best—many students don't have a clue how to start.

"Engaging the Reader" obviously comes before "Providing a Sense of Closure to the Writing." Teachers can add other criteria that target the stages of writing (e.g., prewriting, drafting, revising, and editing successive versions), mechanics, spelling, punctuation, visuals, oral presentation as needed as students progress to the next step. If a student is starting the process, start at the beginning and gradually complete each "chunk" of criteria in a logical order that makes sense. Teacher checklists often become student checklists later on, but usually student checklists are much shorter and would focus on a specific assignment and would not cover all the criteria at once. Teachers can introduce segments as needed with the goal that by the end of the unit, quarter, or semester (and certainly before the state test), the student will have completed everything needed to write an effective narrative essay that meets or exceeds standards.

Figure 3.3

Task: NARRATIVE WRITING CHECKLIST—FOURTH GRADE

Standard: Georgia Performance Standard: English/Language Arts 4th Grade, Writing 2 (GPS ELA4W2)

Criteria/Performance Indicators	Not Taught 0	Taught 1
Engages the Reader		
• Establishes a context		
• Creates a point of view		
• Develops reader interest		
Establishes a Story		
• Develops Plot (fill in the blanks)		
*Who		
*What		
*Where		
*When		
*Why		
*How		
• Develops Setting (fill in the blanks)		
*Where		
*When		
• Develops Conflict (fill in the blanks)		
*Man vs. Man		
*Man vs. Nature		
*Man vs. Himself		
* (select other)		
Creates an Organizing Structure		
• Chronological Order		
• Cause and Effect		
• Similarities and Differences		
• Posing and Answering a Question		

Uses Sensory Language		
• Uses descriptive language		
*Colorful adjectives		
*Vivid adverbs		
• Uses figurative language		
*Similes		
*Metaphors		
*Personification		
*Onomatopoeia		
Includes Concrete Language		
• Uses action verbs		
• Uses appropriate nouns, pronouns, and descriptions		
Develops Complex Characters		
• Portrays realistic protagonist (main character)		
• Portrays realistic antagonist (foil/bad guy)		
• Uses authentic dialogue		
Utilizes Appropriate Narrative Strategies		
• Uses dialogue to drive plot		
• Establishes tension		
• Interjects suspense		
Provides a Sense of Closure to Writing		
• Foreshadows the ending		
• Builds the story to a climax		
• Develops a *resolution* (explanation at the end)		
• Answers key questions		
• Wraps up loose ends		

Figure 3.4

DATA ANALYSIS AND PROBABILITY STANDARD—SIXTH GRADE

Students will represent and analyze data and make predictions from investigations. Students will also demonstrate understanding of statistics by representing, investigating, and using data.

M6D1. Students will represent and analyze data.

    a. Construct frequency distributions, tables, and graphs using data.

    b. Choose appropriate tables and graphs to be consistent with the nature of the data.

Remark: M6D1. Graphics should include pictographs, histograms, bar graphs, line graphs, circle graphs, line plots, and frequency table.

Figure 3.5

Reprinted with permission from the Georgia Department of Education's Quality Core Curriculum. © 2004 Georgia Department of Education. All rights reserved.

see how different teams analyze and de-construct and then re-construct the same standard. Figure 3.5 describes a Data Analysis and Probability Standard for the Sixth Grade.

VOCABULARY LISTS

After analyzing the standard, teachers develop a list of terms they feel the students should know and understand before they introduce the assignment. This vocabulary list can be used diagnostically to determine prior knowledge and the results of the diagnostic pretest could also be used to group students appropriately in order to differentiate instruction (see Figure 3.6). The special-education teachers prefer getting a copy of this list in advance so that they may prepare their students before the classroom teacher introduces the terms in class. The previewing strategy helps students feel more confident and better equipped to complete the assignment.

The conversations teachers have while discussing the various terminology are valuable. Often, the conversations about how to teach specific skills serve as an informal staff development lesson where peers learn from each other. In one district, a group of sixth-grade teachers of mathematics examined the standard and vocabulary list and created a teacher checklist to guide their instruction.

DATA ANALYSIS AND PROBABILITY—VOCABULARY TERMS

Analysis   Graphs

Prediction   Pictographs

Investigation   Histograms

Statistics   Bar graphs

Data   Line graphs

Frequency distribution   Circle (pie) graphs

Frequency/Table   Line plots

Figure 3.6

Team one thought that the standard should be organized and taught in one way in order to be most effective (Figure 3.7).

Team two was also comprised of sixth-grade teachers of mathematics who examined the same standard and vocabulary list and created a different teacher checklist to guide their instruction. Both checklists break down the standard into manageable steps that will guide their instruction and help students understand how to collect, analyze, interpret, and display data appropriately (Figure 3.8).

The final checklist is not as important as the rich conversations that teachers engage in as they analyze the wording of the standard and determine the most effective sequence to introduce the concept to their sixth-grade students. Many teachers use the teacher checklists with their students in order to help them walk through the process. It is often better, however, to develop a similar student checklist (Chapter 5) that asks the same questions but in the context of a real problem that is more specific. Also, student checklists usually focus on parts of the standard as it is introduced. Students, however, should be able to complete all the steps by the end of marking period and prior to the state standardized test.

DATA ANALYSIS AND PROBABILITY—TEACHER CHECKLIST

(Team One)

Standard M6D1—Mathematics—Sixth Grade
Students will pose questions, collect, represent, and analyze data, and interpret results.

	Not Yet 0	Yes 1
Pose Question		
• What data?		
• Who is represented?		
• Which graph to use?		
Collect Data		
• Use frequency table		
• Sample size from population		
Analyze Data		
• Choose appropriate numerical graph		
• Choose appropriate categorical graph		
Construct Graph		
• pictographs • pie graphs • line graphs • histograms		
• bar graphs • line plot		
Interpret Results		
• Relate data analyses to context		
• Relate data to question posed		
• Use graphs to examine variation occurring within groups		
• Use graphs to examine variation occurring between groups		

Figure 3.7

Created by Concetta Archer, Ron Ullman, Susan Wiba, Michele Hoglund, Marily Hall, and Debbie Rhodes from the Muscogee County School District in Columbus, Georgia. Used with permission.

SCIENCE CHECKLIST

Another example shows how a team of sixth-grade science teachers took a very complex science standard (Figure 3.9) and analyzed it. The more abstract a standard, the more important it is to break it down into concrete steps.

DATA ANALYSIS AND PROBABILITY—TEACHER CHECKLIST

(Team Two)

Standard M6D1—Mathematics—Sixth Grade
Students will pose questions, collect, represent, and analyze data, and interpret results.

Elements	Not Yet 0	Yes 1
Formulate Questions to Be Answered by Data		
• Create questions		
• Create survey or experiment		
• Select sample population		
• Conduct survey or experiment		
• Collect data		
Using Data, Construct Graphs		
• Create frequency distribution/table		
• Create graphs		
Choose Appropriate Graph for Data Display		
• Read and create categorical graph—bar, picture		
• Read and create numerical graph—line, pie chart, line plot, histogram		
Use Tables to Analyze Variations		
• Within group variations		
• Between group variations		
• Graphic organizers, Venn diagrams, other		
Relate Data Analysis to Context of Original Questions		
• Write conclusions		
• Make generalizations		

Figure 3.8

Created by Sherree Hatcher, Rosa Patterson, Roslyn Tymes, Dawn Harper, and Beth Johnson from the Muscogee County School District, Columbus, Georgia. Used with permission.

Some scientific vocabulary terms that describe the formation of our solar system are geocentric, heliocentric, big bang, and Milky Way galaxy. The teachers who created this checklist had to reduce the theory and the abstract scientific vocabulary to terms the students could understand. Sixth-grade

SCIENTIFIC VIEWS OF THE UNIVERSE STANDARD—SIXTH GRADE

Standard: S6E1. Students will explore current scientific views of the universe and how those views evolved.

  a. Relate the nature of science to the progression of basic historical scientific models (geocentric, heliocentric, big bang) as they describe the formation of our solar system with the sun at its center.

  b. Describe the position of the solar system in the Milky Way galaxy and the universe.

  c. Compare and contrast the planets in terms of
  • Size relative to the earth
  • Surface and atmospheric features
  • Relative distance from the sun
  • Ability to support life

  d. Explain the motion of objects in the day/night sky in terms of relative position.

  e. Explain that gravity is the force that governs the motion in the solar system.

  f. Describe the characteristics of comets, asteroids, and meteors.

Figure 3.9

Reprinted with permission from the Georgia Department of Education's Quality Core Curriculum. © 2004 Georgia Department of Education. All rights reserved.

students may not all be able to grasp the big ideas in this standard, but the teachers wrote guiding questions and some essential questions that will generate interest among the students. The teachers model the inquiry method and pose higher-order questions that provoke thoughtful reflections and develop interest in even the most reluctant learners.

SPEECH CHECKLIST

Another example of how the specific descriptors from the standards form the basis for the checklist is the speech checklist created from an Illinois Middle School Language Arts standard that asks students to "speak effectively using language appropriate to the situation and audience" (Figure 3.11). Even though speeches or oral communication skills should be consistent across the country, each state, and sometimes each grade level, includes key words that may differ. One of the problems with all the benchmarks, elements,

SCIENCIFIC VIEWS OF THE UNIVERSE CHECKLIST—SIXTH GRADE

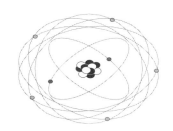

Standard S6E1 – Students will explore current scientific views of the universe and how those views evolved.	Not Yet 0	Yes 1
I. Earth: Where is it? How do we know? How did it get here?		
• Place historical models in correct progression		
– Geocentric model		
– Heliocentric model		
– Current		
• Describe formation of our solar system		
• Nature of science		
Relate how scientists change views (theories) as tools and new information evolve		
• Describe earth's position		
– in the solar system		
– in the Milky Way galaxy		
– in the universe		
II. Earth: Are the other planets like us?		
• Compare and contrast the planets'		
– size relative to earth		
– surface and atmosphere features		
– relative distance from the sun		
– ability to support life		
III. Feel the Earth Move?		
• Explain the motion of objects/relative position.		
– Day Sky—How does the sun move during the day? What is a day?		
– Night Sky—How do the stars move? How do planets move?		
• Explain that gravity is the force that governs motion in the solar system.		
– Why don't we fall off the Earth?		
– How does gravity affect the motions in the solar system?		
IV. Describe the Characteristics of		
• comets		
• asteroids		
• meteors		

Figure 3.10

Created by Kerri Deal, Beth Hendrickson, Patricia Horner, and Janine R. Shingles, from the Muscogee County School District in Columbus, Georgia. Used with permission.

descriptors, or indicators (vocabulary again) is that they are not necessarily listed in any order. Teachers and students often have a difficult time creating a logical organizing structure for the assignment. Notice how some of the items like "aligning content with the characteristics of the audience and the intent of the message" would appear to come first. A student, however, may not worry about aligning the vocabulary, rate, volume, and style until they are much further along in the preparation process. Moreover, they might not even think about those criteria until they begin to rehearse and refine their final speech.

The checklist provides a more sequential or procedural format to help students create, practice, and deliver their oral presentation. Most important, the checklist provides both the teacher and the students a more accurate and fair way to assess the quality of the speech. A speech, by its very nature, is subjective. A criteria checklist takes much of the guesswork out of the grading process and helps "objectify" even the most creative and subjective assignments.

VOCABULARY ACQUISITION

Another example of a so-called "generic" checklist that all teachers can adapt to meet their specific needs includes a vocabulary acquisition checklist developed from an Ohio Standard on Vocabulary Acquisition for sixth-grade students.

A group of sixth-grade educators "dissected" their Ohio Standard on Vocabulary Acquisition and created a checklist that will guide them throughout the year as they introduce key criteria from the standard. The teachers can monitor when they introduce the skill and can also monitor when they assess each skill. The final column shows the date when the students actually master each skill. The teachers feel this tool keeps them focused when they teach and provides evidence when they assess.

This type of checklist could also be used diagnostically at the beginning of quarter, semester, or school year to find out how much prior knowledge students have in the area of vocabulary acquisition. Teachers then know how they will have to differentiate their teaching in order to address the needs of all students. Teachers develop a vocabulary list and use a "Word Wall" for all the terms so that students have a deeper understanding of what they are doing and why they are doing it.

MIDDLE SCHOOL SPEECH STANDARD CHECKLIST

Illinois Standard Stage G-Language Arts

4B-Students who meet the standard can speak effectively using language appropriate to the situation and audience.

(1) Align content, vocabulary, rate, volume, and style with the characteristics of the audience and the intent of the message; (2) employ an engaging introduction, appropriate organization, and an effective conclusion; (3) incorporate nonverbal expressions that are appropriate to the message (e.g., facial expressions, gestures, posture, eye contact); (4) use language that is clear, audible, and appropriate; (5) use appropriate grammar, word choice, and pacing; (6) use notes, outlines, and visual aids; (7) prepare and practice a presentation to fit within a given time limit; and (8) use rehearsal techniques (e.g., taking deep breaths, record or videotape presentation) to practice the presentation.

Criteria/Elements/Performance Indicators	Not Yet 0	Some Evidence 1
Know Your Audience		
• Use appropriate content		
• Use appropriate vocabulary		
• Use appropriate rate (speed)		
Know Your Message		
• Use appropriate content		
• Use appropriate vocabulary		
• Use appropriate rate (speed)		
Organize Your Speech		
• Use an engaging introduction (hook)		
• Use an outline and notes (steps)		
• Use persuasive support statements		
• Use an effective conclusion (closure)		
Criteria/Elements/Performance Indicators	**Not Yet 0**	**Some Evidence 1**
Incorporate Nonverbal Expressions		
• Use appropriate facial expressions		
• Use appropriate gestures		
• Use effective eye contact		
Use Appropriate Language		
• Speak clearly and audibly		
• Use correct grammar		
• Select words carefully		

(Continued)

Use Rehearsal Techniques		
• Practice taking deep breaths		
• Record or videotape presentation		
• Stay within the allotted time limit		
Incorporate Appropriate Visual Aids		
• Use colorful pictures		
• Create graphics to explain key ideas		
• Integrate seamlessly into speech		

Figure 3.11

OHIO STANDARD—VOCABULARY ACQUISITION

Grade 6 Indicators

Contextual Understanding

1. Define the meaning of unknown words by using context clues and the author's use of definition, restatement, and example.

Conceptual Understanding

2. Apply knowledge of connotation and denotation to determine the meaning of words.

3. Identify analogies and other word relationships, including synonyms, antonyms, to determine the meaning of words.

4. Interpret metaphors and similes to understand new uses of words and phrases in text.

5. Recognize and use words from other languages that have been adopted into the English language.

Structural Understanding

6. Apply the knowledge of prefixes, suffixes, and roots and their various inflections to analyze the meanings of words.

7. Identify symbols and acronyms and connect them to whole words.

Tools and Resources

8. Determine the meanings and pronunciations of unknown words by using dictionaries, thesauruses, glossaries, technology, and textual features, such as definitional footnotes or sidebars.

Figure 3.12

ACQUISITION OF VOCABULARY CHECKLIST—SIXTH GRADE

OHIO STANDARD (OHR0602): Acquisition of Vocabulary	DATE Introduced	DATE Assessed	Percent Mastered
Word Structure:			
Identify			
• Root Words			
• Prefixes			
• Suffixes			
• Inflections			
Connection to Whole Words			
• Acronyms			
• Symbols			
Word Structure:			
Apply the knowledge of			
• Root Words			
• Prefixes			
• Suffixes			
• Inflections			
Connection to Whole Words			
• Acronyms			
• Symbols			
Resources:			
Determine the meaning			
• Dictionaries			
• Thesauruses			
• Glossaries			
• Technologies			
Textual Features			
• Definitional footnotes			
• Definitional sidebars			

OHIO STANDARD (OHR0602): Acquisition of Vocabulary	DATE Introduced	DATE Assessed	Percent Mastered
Determine the Meaning of:			
Unknown words			
Context Clues			
• Author's definitions			
• Author's restatements			
• Author's use of example(s)			
Identify and Apply Knowledge of:			
• Denotations			
• Connotations			
Identify and Apply Knowledge of:			
• Analogies			
• Synonyms			
• Antonyms			
Resources:			
Determine the pronunciations			
• Dictionaries			
• Thesauruses			
• Glossaries			
• Technologies			
Textual Features			
• Definitional footnotes			
• Definitional sidebars			
New Uses of Words/Phrases:			
In text			
• Metaphors			
• Similes			
Foreign Words:			
Recognize and use words from other languages that have been adopted into English			

Figure 3.13

Created by Marguerethe Jaede and Sharon Sims, from Columbus Public Schools, at a workshop sponsored by the Central Ohio Regional School Improvement Team (COSIT), in Columbus, Ohio. May, 2005. Used with permission.

Teacher checklists go beyond unpacking the standards. They become a type of "meta-unpacking" because they also help organize instruction. Having a list of nouns and verbs derived from the benchmarks may help clarify the key terms, but it doesn't tell teachers "how" to teach the skill. Teachers may not teach the skills in the order listed on the checklist because of their own teaching style and because of the needs of their students. They do know, however, that they must teach everything before the end of the grading period and before the date of the state standardized test that measures students' academic growth.

APPLICATION ONE

Vocabulary Terms

1. Select key terms from a standard and the benchmarks or indicators.

2. List the nouns (terms, people, processes) students will need to know. Write the definitions for each word.

3. List the action verbs used in the standards. Write the definitions for each word.

4. List the thinking skills students will need to use. Write definitions of the skills. (See Figure 4.5 for list of thinking skills.)

Figure 3.14

APPLICATION TWO

Teacher Checklist

Standards and Descriptors

Select a state standard that you will be teaching. Write or copy the standard and all the descriptors, elements, or benchmarks in this box. Follow the five-step process below to create a teacher checklist. Organize your teaching.

1. Review the standards and descriptions. Write each term on a sticky note.

2. Classify or cluster the terms into groups or headings.

3. Create "holding titles" for big categories.

4. Add terms that will help clarify the process using bullet points.

5. Create a checklist using the template on Figure 3.16.

Figure 3.15

TEACHER CHECKLIST TEMPLATE

Standard: _____

Criteria/Elements/Performance Indicators	Not Yet 0	Some Evidence 1
•		
•		
•		
•		
•		
•		
•		
•		
•		
•		
•		
•		
•		
•		
•		

Figure 3.16

ORGANIZE TEACHER CHECKLISTS

Step 3: Organize Teacher Checklists   How can teachers define key terms from the standards and organize the criteria checklists to guide their instruction?

1. Why do you think organizing criteria into a teacher checklist will help guide your instruction?

2. How can teams of teachers work together to create checklists to share with their colleagues?

3. Why would a vocabulary list be beneficial to students, support staff, teachers, and parents?

Figure 3.17

CHAPTER 4

CREATE PERFORMANCE TASKS

A generation ago, teachers taught a myriad of facts, concepts, and skills to students, and the assumption was that students would then, at some future time and place, use those bits of knowledge to solve problems and to communicate effectively. Today's effective teachers continue to immerse students in the factual knowledge of the various disciplines but take students to the next level by challenging them to use that information to think critically, to create products, or to demonstrate performance in the students' real world of today.

—Stone, as cited in Costa (2001, p. 525)

Definition

A complex performance task challenges students to complete multiple assignments in order to solve a problem scenario. Nitko (2001) says a performance task is a type of authentic assessment activity "that requires students to demonstrate their achievement by producing an extended written or spoken answer, by engaging in group or individual activities, or by creating a specific product" (p. 242). Nitko also believes that a student's performance can be assessed in several ways: by the product the student produces as well as the process the student uses to complete the product. Complex performance tasks transcend activities. They provide a challenging scenario that requires students to engage in interactive and integrated activities in order to solve a problem related to real life.

Wiggins (1998) believes that educators need to focus assessments on "worthy and complete achievement targets—enduring knowledge and competence—and that we must anchor our assessments in worthy, authentic performance problems, tasks, and projects that point towards those targets" (p. 139). He believes these kinds of assessments link schools more closely to the wider world of adult performance.

Rationale

Facts, concepts, and skills provide the essential foundation for student learning. Students need to know important facts from history, key concepts in mathematics, and fundamental skills of writing in order to solve problems, make decisions, and communicate effectively. They need to demonstrate their knowledge and skills on restricted and extended response questions on both teacher-made and standardized tests. However, as Stone (2001) suggests, students also have to use the information they learn to "think critically, to create products, or to demonstrate performance in the students' real world of today" (Stone, as cited in Costa, 2001, p. 525).

Stone discusses how the facts, concepts, and skills—"tools" of math, science, history, or language—are important, but students who are never challenged to "build" anything are short-changed by the educational system. Most real learning experiences demand more than using information and skills related to a single subject content area. Organizing a safety campaign in the school community or preparing for a mock election on campus requires complex thinking and problem solving based on knowledge from multiple subject areas. Students integrate the various subject areas and access the information and skills they need to complete the task successfully.

In addition, research by Kendall, Marzano, and Gaddy (as cited in Strong, Silver, & Perini, 2001) indicates that if teachers "attempt to teach all the standards now in place, the average student would need to add 5 years to his school career" (p. 94). The complexity of performance task units necessitates clustering the standards so that more can be addressed at one time. The tasks also challenge students to work cooperatively to apply their knowledge and skills, to integrate content areas, and to utilize their multiple intelligences creatively to complete the task. Well-designed performance task units motivate students because they correlate to real-life experiences. Students no longer ask their teachers, "Why do we have to do this?" Students who realize there is a reason to study stay focused and motivated.

The following example of a performance task scenario challenges students to use science skills to analyze the Earth's surface, landform identification, erosion, and weathering as well as to use social studies skills to analyze economic concepts and environmental impacts.

"YOUR MISSION"—Science/Social Studies
Performance Task Scenario

You have been selected by NASA to determine the viability of settling an uninhabited area of land on a recently discovered planet within our solar system. Scientists have determined that this new planet, Yopher, is geologically similar to Earth. You will need to assess the planet's natural resources, existing landforms, and the economic and environmental impacts of settlements on those resources. The people of the United States are counting on you to use your knowledge of Earth's processes and economics to determine opportunities for settlement. Be prepared to present your findings and recommendations to the NASA officials on February 3.

Created by Brian House, Scotty McGraner, Brooke Yoder, Courtney Potts, and Elizabeth Ratliff of Edgewood Elementary, Marysville Exempted Village Schools, Ohio. Used with permission.

Performance tasks require students to apply the knowledge and skills they learn to a real problem. Many states include standards for "inquiry methods" to encourage teachers to help students develop problem-solving, decision-making, and inquiry skills and to conduct observations, interpret and analyze data, and

PROBLEM SCENARIO

Write two problem scenarios that would meet the needs of your students.

Problem Scenario #1:

Problem Scenario #2:

Figure 4.1

draw conclusions. Multiple-choice or fill-in-the-blank questions on tests do not provide an adequate assessment tool to measure competencies in these areas.

Performance tasks need to be as authentic as possible and relate to the types of projects people do as part of their lives. In addition, students will want to contribute to the task and create quality work because they will present to an outside audience. In short, performance tasks simulate the types of tasks people do throughout their lives. They require students to think, solve problems, cooperate, and transfer their knowledge by applying what they know. They apply their "book learning" to real life. Moreover, they take pride in creating an original product, project, or performance that showcases their talent and creativity.

Research

The focus on solving real problems in education is not new to educators. In the 1937 publication *Experience in Education*, John Dewey expressed his thoughts about how school should be less about preparation for life and more like life itself. Performance tasks represent inquiry-based or problem-based learning that challenges students to think about and solve realistic problematic situations. Barell (2003) says a "problem" is anything that involves doubt, uncertainty, or difficulty. He says, "We encounter problems of all kinds, from personal to professional, from spiritual to practical. What these situations have in common is that they often cause us to question, to wonder how to solve them, and how to resolve the issue" (pp. 133–134). These problems challenge students to engage their minds and bodies in thinking through "complex, multi-faceted situations where there are no easy, one-word, Scantron-like answers" (Barell, p. 134). Problems necessitate the application or transfer of knowledge—not just the "knowledge of knowledge." Bransford, Brown, and Cocking (2000) (as cited in Zmuda, Kuklis, & Kline, 2004) believe that "Learners of all ages are more motivated when they can see the usefulness of what they are learning and when they can use that information to do something that has impact on others" (p. 261).

Wolfe (2001) discusses how most school goals contain references to developing critical-thinking and problem-solving skills; however, these skills are not always specifically addressed in the classroom. She says that even when teachers give students the opportunity to solve problems, the problems usually have neat convergent outcomes. Wolfe recommends that teachers look for actual problems in their own schools and communities for the students to solve. "These real problems may not be easy to solve because of time constraints or insufficient information, but it is through struggling with these issues that students learn both content and critical thinking" (p. 139).

CHARACTERISTICS OF PERFORMANCE TASKS

The emphasis on performance has manifested itself throughout the United States with the emergence of performance standards. Many states have revised their content-based standards and moved to using action verbs to describe what students should be able to do, not just what they should know. In order to correlate with the recent shift to "performance-based" and "standards-based learning," the colleagues of Benjamin Bloom revised *Bloom's Taxonomy*. Many education majors remember memorizing the six levels of the taxonomy as part of their Education 101 Course, and they may have some problems adjusting to the changes. Upon reflection, however, it seems logical that a person has to synthesize and evaluate all the ideas presented before going to a higher level—to create. Lewin and Shoemaker (1998) describe the characteristics of performance tasks below.

Characteristics of Performance Tasks

Lewin and Shoemaker (1998) feel that a performance task should adhere to the following key characteristics:

1. Students have some choice in selecting the task.

2. The task requires both the elaboration of core knowledge content and the use of specific processes.

3. The task has an explicit scoring system.

4. The task is designed for an audience larger than the teacher; that is, others outside the classroom would find value in the work.

5. The task is carefully crafted to measure what it purports to measure.

From Lewin, L., & Shoemaker, B. J. *Great Performances: Creating Classroom-Based Assessment Tasks.* Copyright (c) 1998 by The Association for Supervision and Curriculum Development. All rights reserved. Reprinted with permission. The Association for Supervision and Curriculum Development is a worldwide community of educators advocating sound policies and sharing best practices to achieve the success of each learner. To learn more, visit ASCD at www.ascd.org

PERFORMANCE TASK TEMPLATE

Key Standards: _____

Problem Scenario:

Whole-Class Instruction: List the content or skills that will be introduced by the teacher to prepare students for the group and individual work.

-
-
-

Group Work: Students may select their group topic or presentation method.

Group 1   Group 2   Group 3   Group 4

Individual Work: Each student will complete the following:

Methods of Assessment: List all the methods of assessment used in this unit:

Figure 4.2

These guidelines form the foundation for developing the performance tasks and merit further discussion and examples.

STUDENT CHOICE

Usually the group projects allow students some choice in their selection of projects or performances. Students choose from a variety of projects using visual/spatial, bodily/kinesthetic, verbal/linguistic, and logical/mathematical intelligences. Choice helps students feel empowered because they usually select something they like and at which they excel. Usually the choices involve projects that target most of Howard Gardner's multiple intelligences. Students may select their group and sometimes their mode of presentation. Groups decide to create a brochure, a poster, a skit, a PowerPoint presentation, or an Internet search to present their information. By allowing students to select their own group and method of presentation, they showcase their strongest intelligence as well as choose something they enjoy doing.

CORE KNOWLEDGE CONTENT

Content and knowledge that are presented in the context of real situations comprise the foundation of effective learning. Performance task units, however, require a more elaborate use of core knowledge as well as the application of specific processes like reading, problem solving, writing, collaboration, or decision making. Students study information in their textbooks, but the knowledge base changes rapidly, and what students learn today could become obsolete tomorrow. However, the transferable thinking skills like decision making, hypothesizing, predicting, analyzing, and evaluating transfer to all content areas and to life. Thinking skills never become obsolete. Moreover, cooperative and organizational skills bridge other curriculum areas and also connect to skills needed in college and work. Very few people succeed in the business world without being able to interact with others collaboratively. Successful people use organizational and responsibility skills to manage their work and the people with whom they work. A powerful performance task unit, therefore, requires students to use their content knowledge as a foundation and then select appropriate products, processes, and performances needed to solve the problem. The task integrates content and knowledge with application.

SCORING SYSTEM

Objective paper and pencil tests do not always capture the complexities of performances, projects, or portfolios, which tend to be more subjective. Performance tasks, therefore, necessitate a different type of assessment tool. Many teachers develop criteria checklists to guide the students in the sequential steps necessary to complete the subjective project. Checklists target the independent variables that often accompany open-ended performances. Instructors later convert the checklists into rubrics in order to provide students with clear expectations for quality work. The rubric helps everyone know "how good is good enough" and provides students and parents with the guidelines they need to deliver not just a product or performance but a quality product and performance. Students will feel more confident about meeting the standards if they know and understand the expectations when the assignment is introduced. Students who have a target and clear guidelines for how to hit the target feel more confident in their learning. They also feel more empowered to work independently in pursuit of their academic goals.

OUTSIDE AUDIENCE

Having an outside audience motivates the students by interjecting some fun into teaching. Instead of writing the task in the third-person behavioral objective format: "The students will write a letter to the editor," the teacher presents the problem scenario by describing how someone urgently needs the students' help in this very important mission. For example, the problem could be stated as follows: "The principal is concerned about the number of complaints he has received from students and parents about the dangerous crosswalk in front of our school. He has asked your class to research the safety issues. You will need to develop a survey to interview students, teachers, and parents about the problems, analyze their responses, prepare a PowerPoint presentation describing the results of the survey, and be prepared to present your recommendations for addressing the problem to the members of the Parent Teacher Association (PTA) at their monthly meeting on January 24. Thank you for your attention to this very serious concern. The safety of all the students at our school is at stake."

Language Arts teachers might be upset by the use of the second person "you" pronoun, but the students know they have been personally "tapped" to solve this important problem and help their principal address the safety issues at the school. The problem is immediate, and the principal desperately needs the students' help. Not only is the problem a real problem, but, hopefully, the students' attempts to solve the problem will be realistic and effective. Performance tasks based on real school or community problems provide students with practical applications for their learning and foster a genuine sense of community in the classroom.

VALID ASSESSMENT

Performance tasks motivate students to learn. Often, however, the performance task units require 2 to 3 weeks of class time because of the variety of individual and group activities and the amount of time needed to prepare and present the projects to an outside audience. The key to the validity of the performance task unit and the justification for the time spent on the unit lies in its correlation to the curriculum goals and the standards. "Covering" each standard separately takes too long and may be almost impossible considering the sheer numbers of standards. Instead of addressing discrete skills measured in "stand-alone" standards, performance task units integrate content, process, and inquiry standards into a "context." Teachers justify the depth of coverage as well as the length of time spent teaching the unit if the unit addresses multiple standards. Life is contextual. When students see the "big picture" of the problem, they recall the knowledge and skills they learned studying content in order to brainstorm the most effective solutions.

Performance tasks may be more prescriptive than pure problem-based learning models that focus on ill-defined problems. Most performance tasks provide a structural approach to learning by allowing students some choice in their selection of process, product, and performance within the framework provided by the teacher. Even though problem-based learning proponents like the multiple problem-solving opportunities of their model, performance tasks do generate some creativity and originality within the standards-aligned structure provided by the teacher. Students explore ways to be creative and original within the guidelines of the structured task and learn how to "think outside the box" in order to achieve Level 4 in the rubric, "exceeding expectations."

Wiggins (1998) feels that "performance or production requires the student to plan and execute a new work from scratch and to use good judgment in choosing apt content and shaping a quality product—a 'synthesis' leading to a 'unique' creation by the student, in the words of Bloom's Taxonomy" (p. 140).

Gronlund (1998) warns that performance tasks take longer than traditional curriculum units. The extra time becomes necessary because of the difficulty of designing the task, the comprehensive nature of the tasks, and the increased time needed to evaluate the results. One teacher reviewed his scope and sequence of curriculum goals for his fourth graders. The teacher decided he could not devote as much time as needed for many of his units. Upon thoughtful reflection, the teacher agreed to take the time to prepare and present a performance task unit if the material was really important or if it were really dull. His guidelines might help others judge when it is the right time to take the time to create a performance task unit.

1. The concepts presented in the unit are so important that in order for students to achieve deeper understanding, they need to engage in an extended performance task unit to help them learn the content.

2. The concepts are important, but the unit is so boring, students would not pay attention unless it was designed to be motivating as well as informative.

The key criteria for deciding about the appropriateness of using performance tasks relate to the concept of authentic learning. Strong, Silver, and Perini (2001) formulated a definition of authenticity to help educators answer "the compelling why" about whether to present a performance task challenge. They regard authenticity as "the curriculum goal in which we help students acquire real-world skills and knowledge by developing their abilities to read, write, solve problems, and apply concepts in a manner that prepares them for their lives beyond school" (pp. 96–97).

If students begin to see the relevance of completing real-world projects or performances, they might finally quit asking the age-old question, "Why do we have to do this?" and teachers may quit answering them by saying, "Because it's in your textbook," or, "Because it's on the state test!" The irony is that the textbook content does not always correlate with the content of the state tests. Therefore, teachers who do not align their curriculum, instruction, and assessment to state standards may have students performing well on their own assessments only to have them score lower on the standardized test. Teachers must target curriculum, textbook, and standards to help students perform well on all the different types of evaluations they will encounter throughout school and life.

The Process

STANDARDS

Performance task units "begin with the end in mind." That is, they begin with the curriculum goals and standards. The unit dictates the content whereas the standards dictate the performances students need to be able to demonstrate they can, in fact, do what the verb in the standard asks them to do. Teams of teachers review the standards and then brainstorm the problem scenarios they present to students in order to motivate them. These teams then need to create some essential questions derived from the standards that students will be required to answer at the end of the unit. Many standards will be addressed in the group activities in the performance task, but the key standards are the ones that all students have to master under the individual work section. For example, if the key standard is "write a persuasive essay to persuade readers to act," then every student will have to write an individual persuasive essay in order to show individual accountability. Standards, such as the ones that follow, can also be addressed either individually or cooperatively in all subject areas:

- access information
- integrate technology
- use multiple sources
- acquire information
- communicate in a variety of formats
- use correct sentence structure
- use correct usage of mechanics
- work collaboratively in groups

Even though teachers address multiple standards throughout the unit, the target standard should be assessed using a criteria checklist composed of vocabulary words from the standards and a rubric composed of descriptors from the checklist. If the target standard requires students to write a persuasive essay to convince students of their view, then every student *must* write the essay. Moreover, the essay should be assessed by the same checklist and rubric to ensure fairness and consistency. The students cannot choose to create artwork, devise skits, develop PowerPoint presentations—and "opt out" of writing the persuasive essay. The other activities constitute a "means to get to the end," but the end result should be a persuasive essay that meets the criteria described in the standard.

HEADINGS AND STANDARDS FOR PERFORMANCE TASK UNITS

Persuasive Essay Performance Task Unit

Unit: <u>The United States</u>   Grade Level: <u>4th</u>   Class: <u>Social Studies</u>   Date: <u>October 2004</u>

Standard: Write a persuasive essay that includes the following:

    o information from research

    o integration of technology into report

    o use of correct sentence structure

    o correct usage and mechanics

Graphing Performance Task Unit

Unit: <u>Graphs</u>   Grade Level: <u>5th</u>   Class: <u>Mathematics</u>   Date: <u>January 2004</u>

Standard: Organize and display data in simple bar graphs by preparing

    o display data in pie charts

    o display data in line graphs

Oral Presentation Performance Task Unit

Unit: <u>Oral Presentation</u>   Grade Level: <u>6th</u>   Class: <u>Language Arts</u>   Date: <u>March 2004</u>

Standard: Use explicit techniques for oral presentations (e.g., modulation of voice, inflection, tempo, enunciation, physical gestures, eye contact, and posture).

Figure 4.3

BIG IDEAS

Although most state standards address discrete skills, teachers tend to focus on topics that are covered in their scope and sequence in their curriculum guides. Topics focus on important areas, but they are not as important as the concepts or enduring understandings that go beyond one subject area. The in-depth nature of concepts allows them to be more universal than topics. Drake and Burns (2004) show how integrated topics correlate to more universal concepts.

As discussed in Chapter 1, the topic of "dinosaurs" can be expanded to the concept of "extinction." Concepts lead to big ideas.

ESSENTIAL QUESTIONS

Just like each unit begins with the end in mind—the standards—so too should a unit begin with essential questions. Essential questions pose high-level questions about the important elements in the unit. Some questions ask the "what" or "who" questions to get at important ideas. Questions that ask "why" or "how" usually necessitate deeper thinking on the part of the student.

Questions like, "Why is there prejudice in the world?" "Why do men go to war?" or "How does nature influence our lives?" generate thoughtful answers that cannot be addressed with a multiple-choice test. Teachers begin a unit by asking the essential questions in order to find out their students' prior knowledge and to motivate them to want to know more about the topic. Essential questions also end a unit when teachers pose the same questions again to find out what the students have learned. Teachers revisit the essential questions frequently throughout the unit and then create additional questions to challenge students to extend their thinking.

TEACHING METHODS

The Performance Task Unit is a curriculum plan that often lasts from two to six weeks, depending on the importance of the material. Even though the unit plan provides the context and the framework, teachers still have to develop daily lesson plans that target each day's lesson. Teaching methods should vary depending on what is being taught and who is receiving the instruction. The following list presents examples of effective teaching methods:

- Direct instruction
- Jigsaw technique

PERFORMANCE TASK
UNIT COVER SHEET

Teacher: _____   Subject(s): _____   Grade: _____

Curriculum Unit: _____

Time Frame for Unit: _____

Primary State Standards: Write the key standards all students have the opportunity to meet. (Individual Work and Assessments)

Secondary State Standards: Write the standards that some students have the opportunity to meet. (Group Work)

Big Ideas of Unit: List the key concepts, enduring understandings, principles, issues, or problems addressed in this unit.

Essential Questions: List three essential questions that guide your teaching and motivate students to uncover the important ideas at the heart of this subject area.

Figure 4.4

- Lecture
- Cooperative groups
- Pair-share
- Inquiry-based methods (or Socratic questioning)
- One-on-one instruction
- Role playing
- Whole-class discussion
- Case studies
- Simulations

THINKING SKILLS

Higher-order thinking skills should be embedded in every performance since the essence of a performance task is problem solving. Solving a problem requires a repertoire of both critical and creative thinking skills. These skills need to be targeted; moreover, they need to be assessed.

RESOURCES

Before beginning a unit, teachers anticipate the resources they need throughout the unit. The textbook serves as an important resource, but often teachers include supplemental books, Internet sites, videos, DVDs, or other sources that may be more current and more appropriate to help students understand the topics and concepts.

SUPPLIES

Interactive teaching requires supplies that allow students to engage in learning. Even older students enjoy the kinesthetic and visual/spatial activities that allow them to be creative. Chart paper, magic markers (especially the scented ones), sticky notes, and brightly colored paper bring out the creative inner child in all students. A collection of supplies allows students to demonstrate their learning through a wide variety of multiple intelligences.

TECHNOLOGY

The demands of the 21st century require today's students to utilize contemporary technology to prepare their presentations. Students enjoy using technologies to showcase their work. When students integrate video streaming

TEACHING METHODS

Teaching Methods: Check the methods that will be used to teach this unit.

- Direct Instruction
- Lecture
- Cooperative Learning

- Inquiry
- Role Play
- Case Studies

- Simulations
- _____
  Other

Targeted Thinking Skills: Check the targeted thinking skills addressed in this unit to target problem solving.

Critical Thinking

- Attributing
- Cause & Effect
- Classifying
- Comparing

- Contrasting
- Decision Making
- Evaluating
- Prioritizing

- _____
  Other

Creative Thinking

- Brainstorming
- Generalizing
- Hypothesizing
- Inventing

- Making Analogies
- Paradox
- Personifying
- Predicting

- _____
  Other

Resources:

- Textbooks: _____ Ch. _____ pp. _____
- Supplementary Books: _____
- Internet Sites: _____
- Videos: _____

Supplies:

- Chart Paper
- Markers
- Poster Paper
- Post-it Notes

- Construction Paper
- Crayons
- Paints
- Scissors

- Tape
- Boxes
- _____
  Other

Technology:

- Computers
- Disks

- VCR/Monitor
- LCD Projector

- Digital Camera
- Scanner
- _____
  Other

Differentiation: List ways you can differentiate the lessons and the assessments by modifying the *content, process,* or *products* to meet the needs of a specific student.

Figure 4.5

and digital photos into their work, they not only demonstrate their creativity but also prepare for skills needed in the workforce. After all, it is difficult to find a meaningful career in the 21st century that does not rely on technology.

DIFFERENTIATION

In today's inclusive classroom, teachers constantly strive to meet the needs of their diverse learners. Differentiation involves welcoming each and every learner by offering change, challenge, and choice to today's classroom. Many teachers differentiate the lessons and the assessments by changing the content, the process, or the product to meet the needs of all their students. Fogarty and Pete (2005) discuss how a teacher changes the content of a lesson to change the complexity of the content and provide various levels of challenge and appropriate student choices.

At the most basic or concrete level of complexity, students use objects to learn. Fogarty and Pete describe how students can work with magnets and other objects to engage in a hands-on investigation. At the next symbolic level, the students view a video about magnets and then draw specific diagrams depicting the direction of the magnetic fields in various instances. At the highest abstract level, textbook readings might be combined with an informative lecture where students discuss the sophisticated concept of gravitational pull.

Fogarty and Pete state:

> To change content complexity, the teacher may set up three stations, each of which uses one of the three tiers for students to experience the learning in a way that suits them. Or, the teacher may actually use all three tiers in a series of lessons. . . . Or, the teacher may simply scaffold all three tiers for the whole class when complex concepts are introduced. (p. 11)

Teachers change the process by moving from direct instruction to cooperative groups to inquiry modes such as problem-based, project-based, or performance-based learning. In addition, teachers change the product by allowing students to use their multiple intelligences to produce a variety of final products such as PowerPoint presentations, brochures, posters, skits, role plays, and case studies that all meet the standards through different media. In addition, teachers differentiate resources and the learning environment to let students determine, as much as and whenever possible, how they can best demonstrate their knowledge of a particular topic.

THE PROBLEM SCENARIO

The problem scenario serves as a hook or call to action to motivate students to handle a problem or a challenge. Although the classroom teacher is really asking the students to perform, the scenario is designed for an audience "larger than the teacher, that is, others outside the classroom would find value in the work" (Lewin & Shoemaker, 1998). Someone other than the classroom teacher needs to be in the audience. With younger students, teachers should contact an outside individual (e.g., a fireman, a local politician, the principal, or a parent) to visit the class so the students can present their information. Often, the students present to another class or to a member of the community who volunteers to visit the class and act as a judge or reviewer who provides feedback to the students. Older students, however, may be more mature and less literal and be more likely to play along with a task that begins, "The president of the United States needs your help. He will be visiting our school . . ." Teachers do not want students telling their parents that the teacher "lied" to them. The age level of the students is a determining factor with regard to developing the scenario. The structure of a performance task scenario usually contains the following:

- Second person "You have been asked . . ." (hook)
- An umbrella task (big picture piece)
- Four or five smaller pieces that make up the umbrella task (usually group work that could be jig-sawed or divided up equally)
- The audience to whom the class will present (outside of class)
- The due date of the final performance

WHOLE-CLASS INSTRUCTION

Before students begin their group or individual work, they need to know the content, skills, or processes necessary. Usually, the teacher introduces or reviews the information using direct instruction or whole-group interactions. Madeline Hunter (1971) identified seven elements of lesson design: anticipatory set, learning objectives, input, modeling, guided practice, feedback, and independent practice. Fogarty and Pete (2005) say teachers can change the order of the elements. "The lesson elements represent the science of teaching, whereas the changes in how the elements are used represent the

(Text continues on p. 92)

PROBLEM SCENARIO

Write two problem scenarios for a unit you plan to teach that would meet the needs of your students.

Select the best scenario for your unit.

Problem Scenario #1:

Problem Scenario #2:

Figure 4.6

WHOLE-CLASS INSTRUCTION

Oral Presentation Example

1. Define key criteria for the oral presentation:

    – Modulation of voice

    – Inflection

    – Tempo

    – Enunciation

    – Physical gestures

    – Eye contact

    – Posture

2. Practice the criteria of an effective oral presentation:

3. View videos of oral presentations:

4. Videotape short speeches and self-assess:

Figure 4.7

WHOLE-CLASS INSTRUCTION

Write what you would present to the class to prepare students for the unit.

Figure 4.8

GROUP ACTIVITY

1. Decide how to divide groups for a scenario you will try; each group performs a different task.

Group Work: Students select the group they want to join.

Group 1	Group 2	Group 3	Group 4

2. Decide how to design a task where each group would complete the same multi-step group project.

Group Work: Each group will do the following:

1.

2.

3.

Figure 4.9

INDIVIDUAL WORK

Select one assignment that each student must perform in order to meet the key target standards.

Individual Work (targeted to primary standards):

Figure 4.10

METHODS OF ASSESSMENT

Describe how you plan to assess each of the assignments (tests, projects, performances, portfolios).

Figure 4.11

art of teaching. Creative teachers craft lessons in ways that are unique and inviting to students" (p. 13). For example, before students begin creating their state brochures to advertise their states, they may need to study different aspects of the state such as geographic areas, major tourist attractions, cultural events, industries, and historical sites.

Before presenting an oral presentation arguing for or against the inclusion of soft drink and snack machines in the school cafeteria, the teacher reviews the components of an effective oral presentation. In this case, the teacher needs to check the state standard to ensure that she covers the criteria listed. The time frame for the whole-class instruction varies depending upon how much new information and skills are presented. If most of the skills have been presented previously, then the review will be much quicker.

GROUP WORK

In order to allow some choice, teachers often let students select the group they would like to join. Sometimes each group does the same activity; other times, each group does a separate activity (jigsaw) that still contributes to the overall umbrella performance task. For example, if students are developing a state brochure, instead of each group researching every aspect, each could specialize in a specific area. The groups could each focus on a separate topic such as sports, cultural events, industries, historical sites, or recreational activities.

In some cases, all the groups are doing the same thing to ensure all students meet the standards and to help coordinate classroom organization. Although the groups may all address the same topic, they can still decide how they plan to research the information or how they plan to present it to the class.

INDIVIDUAL WORK

Teachers know the pros and cons of cooperative group work. The research overwhelmingly supports the benefits of working in teams and learning from each other—but there are several disadvantages. In today's world of accountability, standards, and high-stakes testing, teachers need to know that each student meets the standard. Teachers who assume that all students understand the material often discover otherwise when they grade the students' tests. Sometimes, one or two students do all the work and other students contribute little or nothing to the project. Therefore, each student must demonstrate individually his or her ability to meet the key standard listed at the top of the performance task form. The students may also meet other standards addressed in their group work, but the teacher must have concrete evidence that each student either mastered the standard or is making progress towards meeting the standard. Today's emphasis is on accountability. The teacher needs to make sure "no child is left behind."

METHODS OF ASSESSMENT

In the balanced assessment model, different types of assignments require different types of assessments. Traditional quizzes and teacher-made tests capture a student's knowledge of content; portfolios capture a student's progress and thought; performances and projects showcase a student's ability to apply content and knowledge. It is important to select the most appropriate assessment tool to measure what the student knows and is capable of doing.

Figure 4.12 reviews the components of a performance task unit, and Figure 4.13 provides a template to help organize the task.

Not all performance tasks look alike. Some tasks resemble loosely defined problems that allow students the freedom to search for appropriate solutions. Other tasks provide a framework and supportive scaffolding for students in need of more guidance. Although some students excel when working independently, other students need more support and guidance. Moreover, in today's differentiated classroom, teachers vary the group and individual projects to meet the needs of their regular education students as well as to provide modifications and accommodations for students with special needs.

Two examples of performance tasks show how teachers introduce important concepts. Figure 4.14 shows how kindergarten students communicate with pen pals. Figure 4.15 presents a scenario in which students must take over for a vacationing local weatherman.

Creating a performance task unit is one method to design a curriculum unit. Of course, teachers will probably not develop a performance task unit plan for all their units because it does take more time to plan and to teach. Many teachers try one unit to gauge its effectiveness. It is much more fun when teams of teachers work together to create a unit. Many teachers reserve their judgments until they see their students' reactions. One principal noted the decrease in discipline-related problems when the class was engaged in a unit. Another teacher noticed how involved her special-education students were. The bottom line is that students are motivated to learn, and this, in turn, results in improved academic achievement.

ANATOMY OF A
PERFORMANCE TASK UNIT

Title/Topic: _____   Grade Level/Subject: _____

Standards/Benchmarks: Target power standards that address processes such as writing, reading, problem solving, and technology as well as content standards from social studies, science, mathematics, and language arts.

Task Description:
- Hook/Motivator
- Outside Audience (You have been asked by:)
- Problem Scenario
- Group Work (4 or 5 different performances)
- Due Date

Whole-Group Instruction:
- Direct Instruction
- Readings/Internet
- Guest Speakers
- Videos
- Class Discussions

Small Groups: Selected by Students *(Variety of multiple intelligences)*

Group One	Group Two	Group Three	Group Four	Group Five
Research	Artwork (Poster)	Brochure	PowerPoint	Skit

Other group work

Individual Work: Each student will complete the following:

These must match the standards and should be accompanied by checklists and rubrics.

Methods of Assessment:
- Quizzes, teacher-made tests
- Checklists, rubrics, logs/journals
- Portfolios, interviews, conferences
- Observations

Figure 4.12

PERFORMANCE TASK TEMPLATE

Key Standards: _____

Problem Scenario:

Whole-Class Instruction: List the content or skills that will be introduced by the teacher to prepare students for the group and individual work.

-
-
-

Group Work: Students may select their group topic or presentation method.

Group 1   Group 2   Group 3   Group 4

Individual Work: Each student will complete the following:

Methods of Assessment: List all the methods of assessment used in this unit:

Figure 4.13

PEN PAL PARTY: A KINDERGARTEN EXPERIENCE

Kindergarten Standards: Language Arts—Students use complete sentences when speaking and when describing people. Students speak with peers. Students describe familiar persons.

Problem Scenario: We're having a party! Our new pen pals from a class across town will be visiting us on Friday. We must prepare for the party, so we will need groups to complete the following: (1) create invitations, (2) design welcome poster, (3) draw a map to our classroom, (4) create a cover for our class book, (5) take photographs for our class book, and (6) prepare a list of refreshments. Let's get ready. Our pen pals are arriving on Friday!

Whole-Class Instruction: List the content or skills that will be introduced by the teacher to prepare students for the group and individual work.

- Discuss similarities and differences among the students in class
- Classify students based on characteristics such as age, month of birth, gender, eye color
- Practice writing invitations
- Lead students on a school tour
- Demonstrate and practice using a digital camera
- Read a book about pen pals

Group Work: Students may select their group topic or presentation method.

Group 1	**Group 2**	**Group 3**	**Group 4**
Create the invitation	Design a welcome poster	Draw a map to our classroom	Create a cover for our class book

Individual Work: Each student will complete the following:
Create a self-portrait portraying correct eye and hair color with his or her name written correctly to give to pen pal. Practice introducing one's self to pen pal stating first/last name, boy/girl, age, birth date, hair and eye color while the pen pal uses a checklist to ensure each component is covered.

Methods of Assessment:
Observation
Checklist for each group project
Checklist and rubric for self-portrait and interview with pen pal

Figure 4.14

Created by Robin Goodman and Cheryl Cobb of Metter Primary School, Candler County School System, Georgia. Used with permission.

WHETHER YOU LIKE IT OR NOT—IT'S WEATHER TIME!

Science Standards: 4th grade—Students will analyze weather charts and maps and collect weather data to predict weather events.

Problem Scenario: _____, Chief Meteorologist for Channel 11, is on vacation for one month. He needs a substitute and he has heard about our expertise in weather. He has asked us to present the weather on the 5:00 p.m. news broadcast in his absence. For the program, we will need to (1) use a computer program to create a daily weather graph/chart using appropriate symbols, (2) identify weather instruments and how they are used, (3) collect data from the outdoor weather station, (4) record wind speed and direction, (5) collect weather reports from other media sources. Be prepared to go "live on TV" with our results on _____, 2006. It's weather time!

Whole-Class Instruction: List the content or skills that will be introduced by the teacher to prepare students for the group and individual work.

- Observe/record weather conditions daily on bulletin board chart
- Read a weather-related story
- Watch a science video (e.g., *Magic School Bus/Weather*)
- Review paragraph-writing skills

Group Work: Students may select their group topic or presentation method.

Group 1	Group 2	Group 3	Group 4	Group 5
Use a computer weather program to create a daily weather chart	Identify weather instruments and explain how they are used	Collect data from outdoor weather station	Record wind speed and direction	Collect weather reports from other media sources

Individual Work: Each student will complete the following:
Write a paragraph describing your favorite weather condition and illustrate it appropriately.

Methods of Assessment:
- Observation
- Checklists
- Quizzes
- Rubrics
- Weather Portfolio

Figure 4.15

Created by Jessica F. Brown, Metter Intermediate School, Candler County School System, Georgia. Used with permission.

PERFORMANCE TASK CHECKLIST

Application

Assignment: Review your performance task and self-assess your final product.

Did you include the following criteria?	Not Yet 0	Yes 1
Headings:		
• Title that describes the unit (e.g., "The Nutrition Tradition!")		
• Subject Area/Grade Level		
• Number of state standard (e.g., Math, 3.6)		
• Key words or phrases from standard (e.g., "Adding Fractions")		
Problem Scenario		
• Visuals related to topic at top of page		
• "You have been asked by . . ." hook to motivate the students		
• A paragraph that presents the big picture problem scenario		
• Four or five specific assignments that are part of the umbrella task (brochure, poster, presentation, etc.) that the groups will jigsaw		
• The date the final project is due (e.g., "Be prepared to present on May 2.")		
Whole-Class Instruction:		
• Lectures, textbook, videos, guest speakers, discussions		
• Review of important knowledge, skills, concepts, and processes		
• Introduction of new knowledge, skills, concepts, and processes		
Group Work:		
• Description of four or five different group projects or performances		
• Variety of multiple intelligences addressed		
• Students allowed to choose group or methods of presentation		
Individual Work:		
• Individual accountability to meet primary standards		
• Checklist and rubric provided for students to self-assess work		
Methods of Assessment:		
• Variety of tools (teacher-made test, observation, journal, etc.)		
• Checklists and rubrics using vocabulary from the standards		

How do you feel about your performance task?

Scale
16–19 = A
12–15 = B
7–11 = C
Not Yet

Figure 4.16

CREATE PERFORMANCE TASKS

Reflection

Step 4:   Create Performance Tasks

How can teachers create motivating tasks correlated to curriculum and standards to establish a relevant context for the students?

1. Why are performance task units an effective method of integrating standards with curriculum?

2. How can you differentiate the content, process, and products in the task to meet the needs of all students? Give a specific example.

    a. Standard: _____

       1. Content: _____

       2. Process: _____

       3. Product: _____

Figure 4.17

CHAPTER 5

DEVELOP STUDENT CHECKLISTS

*Self-managing, self-monitoring, and self-modifying
capabilities transcend all subject matter commonly
taught in school and characterize peak performers in
all walks of life. These capabilities make for successful
relationships, continuous learning, productive
workplaces, and enduring democracies.*

—Costa and Kallick (2004a, p. 52)

Definition

Student checklists provide a roadmap so students know the process for completing a complicated task like writing a narrative essay. Student checklists correlate closely with teacher checklists. If the teachers dissect the standard and create a step-by-step process, they incorporate some of the same steps and the same terms on the checklists that they create for their students. Effective checklists list the steps students need to take in sequential order and include the vocabulary words taken from textbooks, class discussions, and the state standards.

By incorporating the exact language of the standards, teachers help students understand the concept, know the key vocabulary terms, and prepare for standardized tests. When criteria are "chunked" or "clustered," the students understand how big tasks are broken down into smaller steps. Basically, a checklist is a mini-item analysis where the teacher "deconstructs" or "dissects" the abstract standard and classifies and sequences the discrete skills into manageable steps. Usually the teacher checklist is too long and is not perceived by students as user friendly because it lists every possible term and criteria used in the standard and accompanying benchmarks. The teacher checklist tends to be generic because it describes the standard in general, but it does not correlate directly to the task the student is working on for the particular unit or assignment.

Criteria, also known as guidelines, elements, indicators, or descriptors, are used to judge responses, products, or performances. When one refers to an assignment being criterion referenced, it means that it is an approach for "describing a student's performance according to established criteria (e.g., she types 55 words per minute without errors)" (Arter & McTighe, 2001, p. 180). Student checklists provide much more user-friendly guidelines because they are often written in question format to guide students through each step of the process.

Rationale

Costa and Kallick (2004b) discuss the importance of students self-directing their own learning. They believe that successful students and adults exhibit the

ANATOMY OF A STUDENT CHECKLIST

Topic /Focus: _____   Grade Level /Subject: _____

Standard/Benchmark:

Name: _____

Criteria: Use vocabulary from the standards and sequence steps in the order students should follow to complete work.	Not Yet 0	Evidence 1
Criterion:		
•		
•		
•		
Criterion:		
•		
•		
•		
Criterion:		
•		
•		
•		
Criterion:		
•		
•		
•		

Ratings

Student's Comments: _____   Total Points [   ]

Scale
11–12 = A
9–10 = B
7–8 = C
Not Yet

Teacher's Comments: _____

Student's Signature: _____   Final Grade [   ]

Figure 5.1

dispositions and habits of mind required to become self-managing, self-monitoring, and self-modifying. Sometimes students modify their learning entirely on their own, but in most situations, they need help. The checklists provide the scaffolding students need as they practice or rehearse the process until they are able to "internalize" the operation and complete the steps on their own. In a typical classroom, a few students will exhibit intelligent behavior and demonstrate that they know, "what to do when they don't know what to do." They know where to look for help and how to access the resources they need to complete the task. Some students need guidance, but are soon able to figure out the correct process and do it on their own with minimal assistance. Other students, however, need extensive help from the teacher and peers in order to complete their work. The effective teacher knows how to differentiate and provide as much or as little help as needed.

Sometimes students approach a task, clarify the outcomes, and gather the relevant data they need to accomplish their goal. These self-managing students draw upon prior knowledge, apply the knowledge and skills needed, and create a viable solution. The goal is for all students to be able to strategize when confronted with complex and demanding tasks. Metacognitive strategies allow students to think about their own thinking and readjust as needed.

Many students, however, need guidance in this process. Students may need an organizational framework to help them navigate the steps, especially if the task involves multiple steps like writing a narrative. Teachers who provide checklists to guide students through the process provide the scaffolding that supports the students' efforts. Once the students practice enough times, they begin to create their own strategies, monitor the effectiveness of their plans, and apply the strategies to future activities and challenges. Eventually, the scaffolding is removed and the building, like the student, stands alone. Not all scaffolding, however, can be removed at the same time. Some structures, just like some students, need different levels of support for different intervals of time.

Research

Baker, Costa, and Shalit (1997, as cited in Costa & Kallick, 2004b) believe that checklists provide guidelines for applying, monitoring, and evaluating performance on specific indicators of self-directed learning. "Students respond to questions that encourage them to develop awareness of their own and others' skills and behaviors, to operate from data rather than from speculation" (p. 52).

In Chapter 3 of their 2001 book, Guskey and Bailey describe how teachers differentiate the types of criteria they use into three categories: products, process, and progress. Process criteria relate not as much to the final results as to how the students arrived at their final product. The Student Research Report Checklist—Prewriting (Figure 5.2) focuses on a standard that asks students to locate, organize, and use information from various sources to answer questions, solve problems, and communicate ideas. It is similar to a prewriting activity that prepares students to write a research report. Instead of the students asking all their questions to the teacher, such as, "Is this a good topic?" "Where will I find something about this?" "What is the purpose of my report?" the students take control of their own learning and follow the guidelines of the checklist to focus them on the key questions they need to answer in order to prepare their report. The user-friendly and age-appropriate questions on the student checklist provide a step-by-step self-assessment so students can check to see if they focused on the topic, found pertinent sources, took notes, and organized information. The teacher "chunks" this one step in a multilevel process. Once the students have all their notes and their outlines, they prepare to write their report.

Process checklists prepare the student for the final product. Sometimes, a rubric is not needed because the checklist is sufficient for describing the work that is required. If the assignment is important, however, the teacher would provide both a checklist and a rubric to ensure quality work.

The process checklist is an assessment tool that allows teachers to include many other factors they value in the students' work. It is not uncommon to include a section on social skills and responsibility at the end of each checklist to make students aware of how well they worked cooperatively in groups to achieve a goal. Process criteria could include questions like the following:

PERSISTENCE

1. Did you write several drafts?

2. Did you check your work for spelling errors?

3. Did you try two solutions to the problem?

4. Did you do your best work?

STUDENT RESEARCH REPORT CHECKLIST—PREWRITING

Standard: Students define and investigate self-selected or assigned issues, topics, and problems. They locate, select, and make use of relevant information from a variety of media, reference, and technological sources. Students use an appropriate form to communicate their findings.

Assignment: Research Report (prewriting)

Did you include the following:	Not Yet 0	Some Evidence 1
Select Topic:		
• Did you choose your topic from the list or obtain approval by the teacher?		
• Is the topic something that will interest your readers?		
• Is the topic something you are interested in?		
Ask Questions and Focus Research:		
• Did you list one or more questions that you want to learn about your topic? What are your questions? _____? _____?		
• Did you look at your questions to decide what the focus of your research will be? What is your focus? _____? _____?		
• Will your research report do one of the following? (1) address an issue, (2) solve a problem or answer a question, (3) tell about someone or something		
Find Resources:		
• Did you use a variety of resources to locate information about your topic? (1) newspaper, (2) magazines, (3) books, (4) Internet		
• Did you check the validity of your sources? 1. publication date _____ 2. point of view _____ 3. primary or secondary sources _____		
Take Notes and Organize Information:		
• Did you take notes?		
• Did you organize and paraphrase your notes into an outline, chart, table, or graphic organizer?		
• Did you select quotations to use in your report?		
• Did you write down all of the information about your sources so that you can document them in your report?		

Figure 5.2

Created by Chris Jaeggi. Used with permission.

SOCIAL SKILLS

1. Did you respect the opinions of others?
2. Did you stay on task?
3. Did you contribute to the group?
4. Did you help others?
5. Did you listen to others?
6. Did you offer encouragement?

Many people, however, believe teachers should give separate marks for social skills, efforts, work habits, or progress. They worry that parents may believe their students are meeting the standards because their grades reflect quality work. The grade could be inflated, however, if the teacher is awarding an inordinate amount of points for using good work habits or practicing appropriate social skills. The parents and the students may think the student is performing on or above grade level. One way to avoid the misconception that a student is doing better than he or she really is on an assignment is to make sure the effort, social skills, and persistence traits are not weighted as heavily as knowledge and performance. If teachers plan to add criteria for "progress" or "process" on their checklists, the criteria should count for a smaller portion of points than the criteria related to the standards-based content. In other words, the criteria used to evaluate understanding of the major concepts and standards should be the focus of the checklist.

When teachers are required to provide a single grade on a report card, they must ensure that most of the grade reflects mastery of content, not behavior, effort, social skills, or participation. Parents and community members who see a single grade of "A" still assume the student has mastered the content. The disconnect occurs when Mary receives an "A" in English based upon a specified criteria of final products, tests, portfolios, process (rough drafts), progress (gains), work habits, effort, motivation, class participation, attendance, punctuality, and daily work. The teacher had described what Mary had to do and communicated those plans directly to Mary, her parents, and the administration. Everyone is proud of how well Mary had done because the grade reflects her ability to meet all the criteria. Red flags quickly arise, however, when Mary fails the state writing test. Moreover, if Mary ends up being retained in the fourth grade, her parents will ask two important questions: Why didn't the system do a better job of preparing Mary for the test? Why weren't Mary's abilities better conveyed on her report card? Were Mary older, she could have received an "A" average in her classes and then score poorly on the ACT or SAT test and not be accepted into the college of her choice. Or, she could make the honor roll and be accepted to a college, only to flunk out in her freshman year because she could not pass English Comp 101. Her parents would begin to wonder how she received A's in her high school English courses. Needless to say, grading is a complicated issue, and the advent of yearly exit exams and state tests has focused attention on the correlation between classroom assessments administered by teachers and standardized tests administered by the state and national testing companies.

Despite the "fairness" of a grading system based upon a combination of assessing product, process, and progress criteria, the reality is that most grade-level exit exams, state criterion-based tests, PSAT, ACT, SAT, and GRE exams measure only two things—product and performance. Although checklists may contain a section devoted to assessing organization, neatness, effort, and teamwork, the focus of the checklist needs to be on content, skills, and concepts. If teachers weight the checklist so that knowledge of the content and performance standards count more heavily than either process and progress, the final grade will portray the students' academic abilities more accurately.

Some schools utilize a two-part reporting system that reports students' ability to meet standards and provides a separate mark for social skills and effort. Blurring the two areas by blending them into a single grade could cause confusion and—in some cases—lawsuits. Despite the importance of focusing on the whole child, self-esteem, effort, and growth, the emphasis in today's schools is on meeting or exceeding the state standards of learning and passing the high-stakes tests required for promotion and graduation.

Criteria checklists provide the roadmap for teachers to plan instruction. Before teachers assign a project or performance to students, they must know the expectations for quality work. Marshall (2003) discusses the "mystery" involved in grading criteria that exists today:

> In many schools, the criteria for getting an 'A' are a secret locked up in each teacher's head, with top grades going to students who are good mind readers. The absence of clear, public, usable guides for scoring student work prevents kids from getting helpful feedback and robs teacher teams of the data they need to improve their performance. (p. 110)

Clear expectations set the benchmark for quality work.

Figure 5.3 helps teachers self-assess their student checklists to ensure they include the key components.

CHECKLIST FOR THE CHECKLIST

Assignment: Review your checklist and self-assess your final product.

Did you include the following criteria:	Not Yet 0	Some Evidence 1
Heading:		
• Title of assignment being assessed by checklist		
• Numbers of state standards and key phrases (e.g., Language Arts 7.6, "Response to Literature")		
• Name of student, grade level, course, or subject area		
• Date of assignment		
Criteria/Elements:		
• Abstract umbrella titles (e.g., "Organization," "Research") that are used for classification but are not graded		
• Bullet points under title ("Introduction," "Body") that are graded		
• Specific directions for students		
• Vocabulary words and synonyms used in state standards		
Scoring:		
• One point assigned for "Some Evidence"		
• Zero points for "Not Yet"		
• Grading scale showing points and final grade earned		
Format:		
• Graphics (e.g., pictures, symbols, clip art)		
• Adequate space for checkmarks and comments		
• Use of vivid colors and bolder print for "Big Categories"		
• Place for signatures		
• Student comment space		
• Checklist arranged in correct sequence of steps		

Reflection:

Scale
15–17 = A
12–14 = B
11–12 = C
Not Yet

Figure 5.3

Creating a Checklist

A checklist may look easy, but several steps go into creating it. In order for a checklist to be valid, it must correlate to the vocabulary of the standards. Many teachers skip the checklist and go right for the rubric, but the checklist provides the formative assessment that prepares students for the summative assessment described in the rubric. The checklist provides a "how to" instructional model that delineates the guidelines for how to complete a project.

For example, students assigned to produce a poster about a country can make sure they are on track to complete the project by answering the following questions:

CONTENT

1. Did you include at least three correct facts about the country?
2. Did you include at least one testimonial about the country?
3. Did you include two tourist attractions?
4. Did you include at least one symbol of the country (e.g., flag, monument)?

VISUAL APPEAL

1. Did you use at least three colors?
2. Did you use an appropriate graphic to represent the country?
3. Did you use key words to capture the attention of the audience?

Student checklists can be formal like the Middle School Narrative Checklist in Figure 5.4, or they can ask questions in a more informal way like the PowerPoint Checklist in Figure 5.5 and the Display Board Checklist in Figure 5.6.

Student checklists are valuable tools that help regular education and special education students alike know the steps they need to take to achieve quality work and meet or exceed the standards. Checklists can help parents to help their children by asking questions about each step.

MIDDLE SCHOOL NARRATIVE CHECKLIST

Standard: The student produces a narrative fictional account.

Criteria Checklist – Clustered and Sequenced

Criteria/Performance Indicators	Not Yet 0	Some Evidence 1
Engages Reader:		
• Sets the context		
• Creates reader interest		
Establishes a Situation:		
• Plot		
• Point of view		
• Setting		
• Conflict		
Creates an Organizing Structure:		
• Topic sentence		
• Support sentence		
• Transitions		
• Motif/theme		
• Symbolism		
Develops Complex Characters:		
• Protagonist		
• Antagonist		
• Dialogue		
Creates Sensory Details:		
• Descriptive language		
• Figurative language		

Figure 5.4

Burke, K., Fogarty, R., & Belgrad, S. (2002). *The Portfolio Connection: Student Work Linked to Standards,* 2nd Ed. Thouand Oaks, CA: Corwin Press. Used with permission.

GROUP POWERPOINT CHECKLIST

Checklist:	Group 2: Create a PowerPoint presentation that displays the scores from each game of your favorite team of the past three years with average yearly scores

Criteria/Performance Indicators	Not Yet (0)	Some Evidence (1)
Technical:		
• Do you have a minimum of five slides?		
• Do you have a variety of graphics, sounds, and transitions?		
• Does it have a professional look with an overall graphical theme that appeals to the audience?		
• Is each slide visually neat, incorporating a variety of layouts?		
• Does it visually depict the material?		
• Does it appeal to the audience?		
• Did you include a graph of the scores from the past three years?		
Communication:		
• Did you use a different form to communicate to the group during the presentation other than the same screen read?		
• Did you maintain eye contact with the group?		
• Did you change your voice during the presentation?		
• Did you check for understanding with the group members?		
• Did you use the allotted time effectively?		
Writing:		
• Did you include a title page?		
• Is it well written?		
• Is it well organized and written in your own voice?		
• Does the material show a strong understanding of the major ideas?		
• Did you include a bibliography?		

STUDENT COMMENTS: _____

_____

_____

Total Points:
Final Grade:

Figure 5.5

Created by Delores Hall, Cynthia Bennett, Martha Williams, Serena Lowe, and Montreal Gore. Tri-Cities/Banneker Cluster. Used with permission of Fulton County Board of Education, Atlanta, GA.

GROUP DISPLAY BOARD CHECKLIST

Standard: Social Studies: Read about and describe the life of historical figures in American history.

Checklist: Group 1—Group Display Board of American Hero

Criteria/Performance Indicators	Not Yet 0	Some Evidence 1
Content:		
• Does your poster have a title?		
• Did you include the historical figure's first and last name?		
• Did you include a picture of the historical figure?		
• Did you include the historical figure's birthday?		
• Did you include the historical figure's contributions in your three sentences?		
• Does your project include a model? My model is _____.		
Mechanics:		
• Did you use common rules of spelling?		
• Did you use correct capitalization?		
• Did you use correct punctuation?		
Apperances:		
• Is your poster 18" × 24"?		
• Did you use at least three colors on your poster?		
• Is your poster neat and free of smudges?		

Reflection:

Grading Scale
11–12 = S
9–10 = N
0–8 = U

Student's Signature: _____

Figure 5.6

Created by Juanita Nelson, Jacinta Alexander, Jacqueline Burnes, LaTrece Crane, Lydia Rice, and Elijah Swift, Hapeville Elementary School. Tri-Cities/Banneker Cluster. Used with permission of Fulton County Board of Education, Atlanta, GA.

MULTIMEDIA PRESENTATION

Students engage in research at every grade level and in every subject area. Any teacher who has taken a class of students to the media center knows how challenging it can be when 30 students wander aimlessly in search of someone to help them. Often the assignment requires students to present a multimedia presentation on their research. The students demonstrate their knowledge of the topic and their ability to communicate using technology.

The following multimedia checklist (Figure 5.7) shows how a fourth-grade student can research weather concepts and prepare a multimedia presentation to the class.

The Research Report on a Country Checklist (Figure 5.8) provides guidance to students as they prepare to write a report on a country. The checklist reminds the students of what type of information they must gather (population, exports, government, tourism, history, topography) while they are in the media center or on the Internet. The rest of the checklist shows students how to organize and write their report. Even though the teacher reviews these requirements orally in class, students sometimes forget! By giving the students the checklist in advance, students can assess if they are on the right track. Whether they are at home doing their homework, working with their parents or a resource teacher, working alone, or collaborating with a group, they know the expectations. The checklist is user-friendly because it asks students to answer questions. The teacher may also provide the students with a rubric based upon this checklist that has key phrases but goes into more details describing the quality that must be included in their work in order to meet or exceed standards (Chapter 6).

The template (Figure 5.9) can be used by teachers to create a checklist for group work. Teachers brainstorm the major holding categories, arrange them in a sequential order so that students know the steps in the process, and then fill in the criteria or bullet points underneath each holding category with vocabulary from the standards. Often, the last section in the group checklist includes cooperation or social skills such as "listening to others," "staying on task," or "respecting the opinions of others."

The template for the student's individual work (Figure 5.10) focuses more on mastering the content, process, and organizational skills. Because each student works alone on the individual work, social skills are not addressed.

CHECKLIST FOR A MULTIMEDIA PRESENTATION

Standard: Communicating with Technology

Assignment: Students will demonstrate their understanding of weather concepts through the creation of a multimedia presentation using (PowerPoint®, AppleWorks® slide show, or Keynote® Presentation)	Not Yet 0	Some Evidence 1
Research		
• Did you use a variety of sources? (newspapers, books, magazines, Internet, or video)		
• Did you use at least 3 different sources?		
• Is your information accurate?		
Content: Do you have information about:		
• At least 3 weather instruments and their uses?		
• At least 4 cloud formations and the weather associated with each?		
• The water cycle?		
• At least 4 weather map symbols and the weather patterns associated with each?		
• At least 5 forms of precipitation?		
Presentation Organization		
• Did you use a storyboard to organize the presentation?		
• Do you have a title slide?		
• Do you have at least 5 informational slides?		
• Do you have a bibliography/resource slide?		
• Have you included audio on at least 2 slides?		
Presentation: Title Slide		
• Does your title catch your audience's attention?		
• Have you included your full name?		
• Have you included the date?		
• Have you included an appropriate graphic?		

(Continued)

(Continued)

Assignment: Students will demonstrate their understanding of weather concepts through the creation of a multimedia presentation using (PowerPoint®, AppleWorks® slide show, or Keynote® Presentation)	Not Yet 0	Some Evidence 1
Presentation: Informational Slides		
• Is your information complete and accurate?		
• Have you correctly edited your text? (spelling, capitalization, mechanics, usage, and grammar)		
• Does your image and audio (if included) enhance understanding?		
Presentation: Bibliography/Resource Slide		
• Have you listed at least 3 different resources?		
• Have you included the sources for your images? (do not include clipart sources)		
• Have you used correct bibliographic format?		
Presentation: Style		
• Is your font style and font size easy to read?		
• Is your text color readable on your background?		
• Is the information on your slide arranged so that it is easy to understand?		
• Is your presentation visually appealing to the audience?		

Total Points: 27

Grading Scale:

24–27 Achieving the Standard
20–23 Progressing toward Standard
19 and below Not Yet

Figure 5.7

Created by Julia Barthelmes and Laura Tucker, Curriculum and Instructional Resource Teachers with Dublin City Schools, OH. Used with permission.

RESEARCH REPORT ON A COUNTRY CHECKLIST

Middle School Standards: Research and organize information using multiple resources.

Assignment: Write a research report on a country.

Self-Evaluation Criteria Checklist: Individual Assignment	Not Yet 0	Some Evidence 1
Research:		
• Did you use reliable sites on the Internet?		
• Did you select a variety of books about your country?		
• Did you obtain information from current periodicals?		
Content: Did you find out information about your country regarding:		
• Population		
• Exports		
• Government		
• Tourism		
• History		
• Topography		
Organization		
• Does your paper begin with an introductory paragraph?		
• Does your thesis statement include three controlling ideas?		
• Does your body include at least three paragraphs—one for each idea?		
• Does your paper contain a concluding paragraph summarizing key ideas?		
Writing Structure:		
• Do you write in complete sentences (i.e., no fragments or run-ons)?		
• Do you use transitions like "moreover" and "furthermore" for coherence?		
• Do you have at least five paragraphs?		
• Do you use a variety of sentence structures (simple, compound, complex)?		

(Continued)

Self-Evaluation Criteria Checklist: Individual Assignment	Not Yet 0	Some Evidence 1
Mechanics:		
• Did you proofread for capitalization errors?		
• Did you and a peer editor check for spelling errors?		
• Did you and a peer editor check for punctuation errors?		
• Did you follow APA style for all your citations?		
• Did you include a bibliography of at least seven sources?		

Did you give credit to your sources by paraphrasing and not plagiarizing? Explain.

What did you find out that surprised you?

What are the three most important things you learned?

1.

2.

3.

What is your goal for your next research report?

Student: _____   **Date:** _____

Comment:

Figure 5.8

STUDENT GROUP
WORK CHECKLIST

Create a checklist for a group project in your performance task.

Criteria/Elements/Performance Indicators	Not Yet 0	Some Evidence 1
•		
•		
•		
•		
•		
•		
•		
•		
•		
•		
•		
•		
•		
•		
•		
•		
•		
•		

Figure 5.9

STUDENT INDIVIDUAL CHECKLIST

Create a checklist for the individual work in your performance task.

Criteria/Elements/Performance Indicators	Not Yet 0	Some Evidence 1
•		
•		
•		
•		
•		
•		
•		
•		
•		
•		
•		
•		
•		
•		
•		
•		
•		
•		

Figure 5.10

DEVELOP STUDENT CHECKLIST

Application

Create a checklist for any project or performance you need to help students complete for either a group or an individual assignment.

Criteria/Elements/Performance Indicators	Not Yet 0	Some Evidence 1
•		
•		
•		
•		
•		
•		
•		
•		
•		
•		
•		
•		
•		
•		
•		
•		
•		
•		

Figure 5.11

DEVELOP STUDENT CHECKLIST

Reflection

Step 5: Develop Student Checklists

How can teachers guide students sequentially through each step in the process of completing an assignment?

1. Why do checklists provide "scaffolding" for students?

2. Discuss the rationale for assigning a grade for a checklist. Why or why not?

Figure 5.12

Student checklists can be compared to training wheels on a bicycle. Many students need a great deal of practice using the training wheels before they ride the bike on their own. Other students may ride a bike the first time they get on without any support. Similarly, some students need the checklist to help them go step by step in a complicated process because they are unable to complete the task on their own. Parents and support staff feel more confident helping students who are aware of the expectations. Similarly, students who prefer independent work can work at their own pace and not only ride the bike, but also enter a race.

Teachers who create user-friendly checklists with steps listed in sequential order empower students to take control of their own learning. They also provide students a mechanism by which to self-assess their own work and set new goals for improving their academic achievement, with or without the training wheels. Let the race begin!

CHAPTER 6

DESIGN TEACHING RUBRICS

We must constantly remind ourselves that the ultimate purpose of evaluation is to have students learn to become self-evaluative. When students graduate from our schools, we want them to have methods of self-evaluation and to know how to turn to external critique for self-improvement. We want them to know how to give and receive constructive feedback and how to revise their work based upon such feedback.

—Costa and Kallick (2004a, p. 3)

Definition

The word "rubric" in the field of education refers to a scoring guide designed to provide constructive feedback to students by helping them think more clearly about the characteristics of quality work. A rubric is designed to show how important elements of a task would look in a progression from less well developed to exceptional along a continuum (Tomlinson, 2003). The word "rubric" comes from Latin and it means "red." Catholic liturgy and law books used red print to delineate important ideas that deserve attention. Today, rubrics refer to print descriptions of performance behaviors that mark the intervals or comparative characteristics and provide evidence that a certain level of performance has been attained. Solomon (1998) defines a rubic as "an assessment tool that verbally describes and scales levels of student achievement on performance tasks" and adds that "it can also be associated with more conventional alpha numeric and numeric scores or grades" (p. 120). Rubrics based upon state standards with scaled descriptive levels of progress toward the standard offer valid feedback regarding how well a student is doing at any given point in time. Most important, in order for a rubric to be valid, it has to be correlated to the standards. Vocabulary from the standards and benchmarks must be embedded in the descriptors.

Rubrics define the expectations for a learning task and assign values to each level of quality—usually ranging from a low score of "1" to a high score of "4." Nelson and Lindley (2004) believe that rubrics represent a clear and easy way to communicate not only the "what" of a learning task, but also the "how" and "how well." They tell teachers to "think of a rubric as an advanced organizer for students—a way of getting feedback before they even begin their project or task" (p. 104). Nelson and Lindley also recommend teachers create and use rubrics as advanced organizers for their own teaching. Teachers who "begin with the end in mind" keep the learning goals in focus and plan their lessons to achieve the goals and to help students improve their performance. Various types of rubrics are available in books and from Internet sites; however, analytical rubrics correlated to the criteria in each state's standards provide the clearest "advanced organizers" for teachers and students. Figure 6.2 shows guidelines for developing a valid rubric that provides the most pertinent feedback.

Depka (2001) shows how the descriptors repeat themselves and new descriptors are added to each score in a natural progression. The steps that

ANATOMY OF A RUBRIC

Topic/Focus: _____   Grade Level/Subject: _____

Standard:

NAME: _____

Ratings

Criterion	1 Novice	2 Approaching Standards	3 Meets Standards	4 Exceeds Standards	Score
Criterion • • •		**Descriptors of Quality**			— × 5 — (20)
Criterion • • •					— × 5 — (20)
Criterion • • •					— × 5 — (20)
Criterion • • • •					— × 5 (20)
Criterion • • • •					— × 5 — (20)

Student's Comments: _____   Total Points [   ]

Teacher's Comments: _____

Scale
90–100 = A
80–89 = B
70–79 = C
Not Yet

Figure 6.1

BURKE'S GUIDELINES FOR RUBRIC

Rubrics are most effective when teachers utilize the following criteria:

1. Use specific numbers like "2" or "3 or more" rather than vague words like "some," "many," or "few."

2. Use specific descriptors like "original," "novel," "vivid," rather than "good," or "excellent."

3. Use the vocabulary of the standards and benchmarks to make rubrics valid.

4. Arrange the scores of the scale on a continuum from 1 to 4 with an equal interval between each score.

5. Use the score of "3" to show students meet the state standard, and a score of "4" to show students exceed the standard by doing exceptional work.

6. State clear expectations for work so that all teachers, students, and parents know the criteria for quality and the requirements for earning a grade.

Figure 6.2

RUBRIC STARTERS

Kindergarten Math: Geometry and Spatial Sense: Recognize, name, and sort geometric figures – triangles

	Novice 1	In Progress 2	Meets Standards 3	Exceeds Standards 4
Shape Recognition "Triangle"	Student can: • recognize and name the triangle by shape	Student can: • recognize and name the triangle by shape • **draw a triangle**	Student can: • recognize and name the triangle by shape • draw a triangle • **find triangles in the "real world"**	Student can: • recognize and name the triangle by s shape • draw a triangle • find triangles in the "real world" • **state characteristics of the triangle**

Figure 6.3

Created by Eileen Depka (2002), Waukesha School District, Waukesha, Wisconsin. Used with permission.

kindergarten students take to recognize a triangle reflect developmentally appropriate progress. As students get older, it is not necessary to repeat the previous step since they cannot earn the higher rating until they have mastered the ones before it.

Rubrics generally specify categories of significance in achieving quality. Sometimes they appear on a Likert scale with equal intervals between each score. They also contain specific categories for the criteria that are required. For example, a research report could address categories that include: accuracy of information, persuasiveness, credibility of sources, organizational flow, and objectivity. Tomlinson and Edison (2003) believe that the most effective rubrics help students explore qualitative differences in their work, rather than quantitative differences. The authors note that "it is not necessarily an indication that a student has done better work if he or she used five resources rather than four. A more appropriate indication of quality is that the student synthesized understandings from several reliable resources" (p. 238). In other

RUBRIC FOR A QUOTATION

Quotation	①	②	③	④
Student includes an appropriate quotation to support research	• includes a quotation • cites author	• cites title of author (president of FDA, scientist, board member)	• cites the source (*Newsweek*) • cites the date	• supports the arguments • is punctuated correctly

Figure 6.4

words, quantity does not necessarily equate to quality. The student could use five resources, but they could be 10 years old, taken from a dubious Internet site, or based upon unsubstantiated facts or speculations.

Students could include one quotation or five quotations, but the five quotations may not be appropriate. Figure 6.4 shows how a quotation can be judged. Many students obsess over numbers with regard to grading and ask questions such as: "How many pages does it have to be?" "How many bibliographic entries do we need?" and "How long does the outline have to be?" The challenge will be in helping students to switch their mindset and their questions from "How many quotes do I need to get an A?" to "Will this quotation help me prove my point?" One of the goals for using rubrics is to help students internalize the criteria for excellence and become critical self-assessors of their own work. Hopefully, students will stop playing the "numbers" game and switch instead to the "quality" game so they can answer their own question of "How good is good enough?"

Holistic Rubrics

Most rubrics use a rating scale ranging from 0 to 3, 1 to 4, or 1 to 6. Depka (2001) states the scale of 1 to 4 is probably the most common because it encompasses a wide range of quality descriptors that do not overwhelm the students. Holistic rubrics have one performance expectation description at each numerical level on the rubric. The product or performance is evaluated as a

ORAL PRESENTATION
HOLISTIC RUBRIC

Name: _____   **Date:** _____

Subject: _____   **Final:** _____

5	The subject is addressed clearly Speech is loud enough and easy to understand Good eye contact Visual aid is used effectively Well-organized
4	Subject is addressed adequately Speech has appropriate volume Eye contact is intermittent Visual aid helps presentations Good organization
3	Subject is addressed adequately Speech volume is erratic Student reads notes – erratic eye contact Visual aid does not enhance speech Speech gets offtrack in places
2	Speech needs more explanation Speech is difficult to understand at times Lack of adequate eye contact Poor visual aid Lack of organization
1	Speech does not address topic Speech cannot be heard Very little eye contact No visual aid No organization
	Scale: 5 = A; 4 = B; 3 = C; 2 = D; 1 = Not Yet **General Comments:**

Figure 6.5

Burke, K. (2005). *How to Assess Authentic Learning,* 4th Ed. Thousand Oaks, CA: Corwin Press. Used with permission.

whole and is often given a single score. McTighe and Wiggins (1999) describe how the holistic rubric is used "to obtain the overall impression of the quality of a performance or product" (p. 277). Popham (1999) says the evaluator will make a single overall judgment about a student's response by considering all of the rubric's evaluative criteria. The virtue of holistic scoring is that it is quicker to write and to use. Holistic rubrics are usually summative because they evaluate work at the end of the process. They are used at the end of a course or to grade standardized writing assessments. The downside of holistic scoring, Popham notes, is "that it fails to communicate to students, especially low-performing students, what their shortcomings are" (p. 167).

Analytical Rubrics

Analytical rubrics use multiple descriptors for each criterion evaluated within the rubric. In essence, the student's product contains multiple opportunities to be evaluated within the same rubric (Depka 2001). It is a type of "task analysis" where teachers award response points on a criterion-by-criterion basis. Popham (1999) says that "clearly, analytical scoring yields a greater likelihood of diagnostically pinpointed scoring and sensitive feedback than does holistic scoring" (p. 167). Analytical rubrics have been described as "teaching rubrics" because their design helps students improve their own performance. Teaching rubrics are formative assessments because they provide continuous feedback to students and teachers about progress students make towards achieving goals. Analytical rubrics provide ongoing assessment that is integrated with instruction in a continuous feedback loop that allows teachers to refocus instruction on an ongoing basis.

The checklist for a letter to the editor in Figure 6.6 shows how the students know the criteria for a quality letter. Teachers can convert the checklist to a rubric (Figure 6.7) by using the same criteria and adding descriptors of quality.

Solomon (2002) notes that although politicians and educators may be interested in holistic scores, "it is the analytical potential of rubrics, their ability to pinpoint specific gaps or deficiencies, that may be most useful to the school improvement process" (p. 63). Analytical rubrics target areas of weakness and help parents and teachers focus on the specific criteria a group of students or an individual student needs to master in order to meet or exceed standards and pass the summative evaluation.

LETTER TO THE EDITOR CHECKLIST

Standard: Students will write a letter to the editor to persuade people about an issue.

Indicators—Persuasive Writing	Not Yet (0)	Some Evidence (1)
Accuracy of Information		
• Facts		
• Statistics		
Persuasiveness		
• Logic		
• Examples		
• Quotations		
Organization		
• Topic Sentence		
• Support Sentences		
• Concluding Sentence		
Usage		
• Grammar		
• Sentence Structure		
• Transitions		
Mechanics		
• Capitalization		
• Punctuation		
• Spelling		
Letter Format		
• Date		
• Inside Address		
• Salutation		
• Body		
• Closing		
• Signature		

Scale:
18–20 = A
16–17 = B
14–15 = C
Not Yet

Total Points: [   ]

(out of 20)

Final Grade: _____

Figure 6.6

LETTER TO THE EDITOR RUBRIC

Standard: Students will write a letter to the editor to persuade people about an issue.

Scoring Criteria	1 Rejected by Church Bulletin Committee	2 Published in High School Newspaper	3 Published in Local Newspaper	4 Published in The New York Times	5 Score
Accuracy of Information • Facts • Statistics	3 or more factual errors	2 factual errors	1 factual error	All information is accurate and current	___ × 4 ___ (16)
Persuasiveness • Logic • Examples • Quotations	• Illogical • No examples • No quotations	• Faulty logic • 1 example • 1 quotation	• Logical arguments • 2 examples • 2 quotations	• Logical and convincing arguments • 3 examples • 3 quotations	___ × 4 ___ (16)
Organization • Topic Sentence • Support Sentences • Concluding Sentence	• Includes 1 element • Fragmented	• Includes 2 elements • Lacks coherence	• Includes all 3 elements • Logical	Includes all 3 elements • Logical • Coherent	___ × 4 ___ (16)
Usage • Grammar • Sentence • Structure • Transitions	4 or more errors (distracts from arguments)	2–3 errors (weakens case)	1 error (structure reinforces arguments)	No errors (structure informs and convinces reader)	___ × 4 ___ (16)
Mechanics • Capitalization • Punctuation • Spelling	4 or more errors (destroys credibility)	2–3 errors (weakens case)	1 error (careless proofreading)	Accurate mechanics (polished and professional)	___ × 4 ___ (16)
Letter Format • Date • Inside Address • Salutation • Body • Closing • Signature	• Includes 3 elements	• Includes 4 elements	• Includes 5 elements • Correct spelling	• Includes 6 elements • Correct punctuation	___ × 4 ___ (16)

Comments: (Worth 4 Points)

Scale
A = 92–100
B = 85–91
C = 77–84
D = 70–76

Final Score: _____
(96)

Final Grade: _____

Figure 6.7

The Analytical Rubric for Narrative Writing (Figure 6.8) can be used as a diagnostic tool to measure each student's ability to write a narrative fictional account at the beginning of the year. The same rubric can be used throughout the year to measure students' progress.

The analytical rubrics in this chapter provide detailed feedback to students about the specific criteria they need to address in order to improve their performance. Feedback helps students know exactly what they have to do to meet and exceed standards and complete assignments correctly.

Rationale

Why do we need rubrics to evaluate student work? How many parents of today's students know the word "rubric" and understand why rubrics have become essential tools for assessing student work? Parents at back-to-school night or during parent-teacher conferences have remarked, "We didn't have rubrics when we were going to school, and we turned out okay" or "The rubrics are fine, but what did he really get for a grade?" How can teachers explain the purpose of using rubrics so that all the stakeholders see their value?

Effective analytical rubrics provide specific feedback to improve the quality of a student's work. Guskey and Bailey (2001) believe that regularly checking on students' learning progress is an essential aspect of successful teaching. In order to facilitate learning, teachers need to provide students with regular and specific feedback on their learning progress. They believe that feedback must be paired with "explicit guidance and direction for making improvements when needed" (pp. 30–31). Rubrics help provide specific feedback because they describe what the student needs to do to move from a score of "2" to a score of "3" in order to improve to meet the standard. Many states also require teachers to provide commentary to students about their work. Some teachers add a "teacher comment" section at the end of a rubric so they can encourage the student to set a new goal to improve performance. The Research Report on a Country Checklist in Chapter 5 (Figure 5.8) provides a question to guide students. If the teacher wants to extend the checklist to a rubric in order to provide more descriptors to describe quality and provide a grade, she can use key words from questions and insert them into the Research Report on a

ANALYTICAL RUBRIC
FOR NARRATIVE WRITING

Middle School English Language Arts Standard: The student produces a narrative fictional account.

Criteria The student:	1 Below the Standard	2 Approaching the Standard	3 Meets the Standard	4 Exceeds the Standard	Score
Engages the Reader					
Context	No context	Context is confusing	Context sets the scene for the story	Context develops a framework for the story	
Reader interest	Does not engage reader	Attempts to engage reader	Captures the reader's attention	Grips the reader's attention	
Establishes a Situation					
Plot	No evidence of plot	Plot is confusing	Plot is coherent	Plot provides surprising twists	
Point of View	Vague point of view	Shifts from 1st, 2nd, and 3rd person	Shifts from 1st person to 3rd person	Uses appropriate point of view consistently	
Setting	Not provided	Provides place or time	Provides place and time	Vividly describes both place and time	
Conflict	No conflict	Rising action	• Rising action • Climax	• Rising action • Climax • Denouement	
Creates an Organizing Structure					
Topic Sentence	None	Wrong main idea	Correct and controlling main idea	Clear and powerful controlling main idea	
Supporting Sentences	Sentences do not relate to topic sentence	1 supporting sentence related to topic	2 supporting sentences related to topic	3 or more well-written supporting sentences	
Transitions	No transitions	Basic transitions (and, but . . .) used appropriately	Varied transitions (however, moreover, therefore . . .) used	Skillful use of transitional words and phrases to connect ideas	

Criteria The student:	1 Below the Standard	2 Approaching the Standard	3 Meets the Standard	4 Exceeds the Standard	Score
Motif/Theme	No evidence	Vague theme— not fully developed	Theme woven throughout	Theme appropriately conveys author's message	
Symbolism	No symbols	Vague use of 1 symbol— not fully developed	1 to 2 appropriate symbols woven throughout	1 to 2 effective symbols that contribute significantly to the meaning of the story	
Develops Complex Characters					
Protagonist	Not fully developed	Stereotypical "good guy" (no surprises)	Fully developed main character	Complex and empathetic main character	
Antagonist	Not fully developed	Stereotypical "bad guy" (no surprises)	Fully developed foil to main character	Complex foil to main character	
Dialogue	Little or no dialogue among characters	Stilted dialogue that does not fully develop characters	• Realistic dialogue appropriate to characters • Advances plot line	• Colorful dialogue • Use of appropriate dialect, idioms, or slang	
Creates Sensory Details					
Descriptive Language	Lacks specific descriptions	Word choice is bland and/ or nondescript	Use of descriptive adjectives	Use of vivid descriptive words that "paint a picture" in the mind	
Figurative Language	No figurative language	Use of simile or metaphor	Use of simile and metaphor	Use of personification or onomatopoeia	
Concrete Language	Nondescript language	Use of appropriate language	Use of action verbs and concrete nouns	Use of vivid words that enhance narrative	

Closure	1	2	3	4	
Foreshadowing	No evidence	1 obvious hint	1 subtle hint	2 or more clever hints	
Story Ending	• No ending or inappropriate ending • No foreshadowing	• Unsatisfying ending • Loose ends • Weak foreshadowing	• Ending provides closure to story • Evidence of foreshadowing	• Cleverly foreshadowed surprise ending	

Comments: _____

_____

_____

_____

_____

_____

Signed: _____

Date: _____

Scale
67–72 = A
48–6 = B
28–7 = C
0–27 = D-F
Not Yet

Figure 6.8

Country Rubric template (Figure 6.9). Once the same criteria on the checklist are plugged into the rubric template, the teacher can write descriptors of quality in each cell to extend the checklist into a rubric.

Teachers utilize rubrics to guide students through the learning process and to evaluate their work fairly and consistently. Instructional rubrics provide the scaffolding to help students self-regulate their work. Saddler and Andrade (2004) discuss the importance of having student involvement in creating an instructional rubric for writing. They believe that teachers commonly use assessment rubrics to score and grade student work but they believe "instructional rubrics are often created with students and are always written in language that students can understand" (p. 49).

Teachers who create instructional rubrics before the students begin the writing process empower them to plan, revise, and edit their own work. Even though many teachers attempt to provide continuous feedback throughout the writing process, it is sometimes impossible to have one-on-one conferences with each student or to write specific remarks on each rough draft because of the number of students in a class. A teacher's goal of providing individual feedback throughout the writing process is often hampered in classrooms containing 35 students. However, if all students in the class know the criteria for quality writing, they serve as "critical friends" or "reflective critics" as they peer-edit each other's work. Students internalize the criteria for quality work when they teach others. Saddler and Andrade (2004) believe that the quantity of feedback that a writer receives throughout the writing process contributes to a well-crafted piece of writing. They believe that "student assessment has the additional advantage of promoting self-regulation because it gives students some of the responsibility for judging written work instead of placing that responsibility solely on the teacher" (p. 51). Because of the preciseness of the descriptors, it takes more time to develop instructional rubrics. The Analytical Rubric for Narrative Writing (Figure 6.8) shows how students can monitor their own progress. Once the rubrics are developed, however, teachers and students become more skillful at assessing the specific criteria inherent in a quality piece of work. Moreover, teachers become more consistent and fair in their grading process and students become more consistent and fair in their self-assessment of their work.

Black, Harrison, Lee, Marshall, and William (2004) believe that teachers should take time to help students understand scoring rubrics so that they either rewrite them or create their own. They believe that "students' reflection

RESEARCH REPORT
ON A COUNTRY RUBRIC

SCALE:	1	2	3	4
Research • Internet Sites	• Use of 1 Internet site • Not credible	• Use of 2 Internet sites • Credible sources	• Use of 3 Internet sites • Credible sources • Pertinent information	• Use of 4 or more Internet sites • Credible sources • Pertinent information • Current information
• Variety of Books (biography, encyclopedia, almanac, atlas)	• 1 type of book	• 2 types of books	• 3 types of appropriate books	• 4 types of appropriate and current books
• Current Periodicals	1 periodical	2 periodicals	3 periodicals	4 or more current periodicals
Content • Population	Included	Explained	Analyzed	Evaluated
• Exports	Included	Explained	Analyzed	Evaluated

SCALE:	1	2	3	4
CRITERIA:				
• Government	Included	Explained	Analyzed	Evaluated
• Tourism	Included	Explained	Analyzed	Evaluated
• History	Included	Explained	Analyzed	Evaluated
• Topography	Included	Explained	Analyzed	Evaluated
Organization				
• Introductory Paragraph	None	Introduced main idea	Introduced 3 controlling ideas	Hooked the reader
• Body	1 paragraph	2 paragraphs	3+ paragraphs	Coherent transitions
• Concluding Paragraph	None	Summarized key ideas	Referred back to introduction	Memorable closure

Figure 6.9

CHECKLIST/RUBRIC TEMPLATE

Standards: _____

SCALE:	1	2	3	4
CRITERIA:				
[ ] •				
•				
•				
[ ] •				
•				
•				
[ ] •				
•				
•				
[ ] •				
•				
•				

Figure 6.10

about their understanding can also be used to inform future teaching, and their feedback can indicate in which areas a teacher needs to spend more time" (p. 15). Another type of rubric that focuses more weight on the key standards or the areas emphasized by the teacher is the weighted rubric. Figure 6.11 shows how a teacher could weight a rubric to show students that some criteria are more important than others. Students would want to do a thorough job writing their reflections since they count for 28 points. Focus should be on the key standard and understanding—not necessarily on spelling.

Data provide information that improves a teacher's ability to make informed and reasoned decisions. Conzemius and O'Neill (2001) believe that when teachers reflect on student performance data, like the data described in a rubric, they receive valuable feedback about the nature and the extent of the impact they are having on their students. "They know that what they are doing is making a difference. Without the feedback data provides, teachers can only guess (and hope) that their students have achieved the desired outcomes" (p. 47). Rubrics provide more valuable feedback to students and parents because they provide a more objective analysis of student performance. Grades of A, B, C, and "Satisfactory" or "Passing" do not give people specific indications of what the student needs to do to improve.

Littky (2004) believes that schools use grades just because someone once decided on it and everybody simply continues to go along with it—except in the real world. He believes adults in the real world are given real feedback that includes indications of where they need to improve. Littky offers a compelling argument:

> In the real world, when we evaluate things, we talk about the specifics of what is right and what is wrong. A baseball coach doesn't say to his player, 'You earned a B today.' He says, 'You took your eye off the ball today. You need to concentrate more. You need to change your stance.' The real world is built around giving feedback and showing people what they need to do to improve. And yet in schools, we hand out single-letter grades and think nothing of it. (p. 154)

A standards-based rubric (Figure 6.12) shows that students must go "beyond" the standard to receive an "A." Many districts cannot decide whether the "3" meets the standards or the "4" meets the standards. Because the word standard denotes "satisfactory," it seems that students need to go above and beyond that to exceed the standards and earn an "A."

WEIGHTED RUBRIC FOR PORTFOLIO

Student: _____   Subject: _____

Date: _____

Goal/Standard: Use reading writing, listening, and speaking skills to research and apply information for specific purposes.

Criteria	Indicators	1	2	3	4	Score
Form	• **Spelling** • **Grammar** • **Sentence structure**	2-3 errors	1-2 errors	0 errors	0 errors and a high level of writing	__ × 3 __ (12)
Visual Appeal	• **Cover** • **Artwork** • **Graphics**	Missing 3 elements	Missing 1 element	All 3 elements included	All 3 elements are creatively appealing	__ × 4 __ (16)
Organization	• **Completeness** • **Timeliness** • **Table of contents**	Missing 2 elements	Missing 1 element	All 3 elements included	All 3 elements demonstrate high level of organization	__ × 5 __ (20)
Knowledge of Key Concepts	• **Key concepts** • **Evidence of understanding** • **Application**	Evidence of key concepts included in portfolio	Evidence of basic level of under-standing of key concepts	Evidence of high level of under-standing of key concepts	Evidence of ability to apply knowledge to new situations	__ × 6 __ (24)
Reflections	• **1 per piece** • **Depth of reflection** • **Ability to self-assess**	Missing 2 or more reflections	Missing 1 reflection	Insightful reflections for each piece	Reflections show insightful-ness and ability to self-assess	__ × 7 __ (28)

Scale
A = _____
B = _____
C = _____
D = _____

Final Score: _____
(100)

Final Grade: _____

Comments:

Figure 6.11

Burke, K. (2005). *How to Assess Authentic Learning,* 4th Ed. Thousand Oaks, CA: Corwin Press. Used with permission.

STANDARDS-BASED RUBRIC TEMPLATE

Standard: _____

Criteria The student:	1 Below the Standard	2 Approaching the Standard	3 Meets the Standard	4 Exceeds the Standard	Score

Figure 6.12

Rubrics foster student independence. Costa and Kallick (2004) believe that independent and self-directed learners demonstrate a commitment to change by building critique and assessment into their everyday actions:

> By reexamining and clarifying various aspects of the values, purposes, goals, strategies, and outcomes, they continue to learn and develop an even more positive disposition towards continued learning. (p. 7)

An objective test may be appropriate for factual knowledge in which questions have a single right answer, student responses can be tallied, and percentages calculated. But for more complex instructional goals, and for assessment methods that do not yield a single correct response, an assessment must have a predetermined scoring system for evaluating student work. Danielson (1996) discusses how a rubric not only identifies the criteria of an acceptable response but also establishes standards of performance. She believes that students "should know the required standards of achievement because secrecy has no role in assessment—such an environment feels like 'gotcha' to students" (p. 76). Various rubric templates allow teachers to determine which format works best for an assignment. Figure 6.13 is a "Rubric Checklist" that teachers can use to self-assess their rubrics to ensure they have met the criteria for developing a quality rubric.

Tomlinson (2003) discusses how a rubric can be either task specific (in order to help students plan and evaluate a particular piece of work) or generic (to be used repeatedly during a course or year to help students in a variety of subjects or repeatedly in a single subject). Rubrics come in all shapes, sizes, and types and can be utilized for many different purposes. Even though Latin phrases are not used as frequently in today's classroom, and rubrics are not always "red," rubrics continue to focus on important ideas that deserve attention. Despite the work involved, teams of teachers who collaborate can transform their teacher checklists into appropriate student checklists.

Once they have determined that all the criteria from their curriculum and the standards are embedded in the checklists, teachers extend the checklists into rubrics. The difficult task is to write clear descriptors, use bullet points, and describe exactly what constitutes each score in each cell of the rubrics. The creation of the rubric completes the six-step cycle. The process that began by targeting the standard in step one ends by assessing the standard in step six.

Teams of teachers begin by targeting the standards and then move through each of the steps until they create the final rubrics. The rubrics tell teachers how well they taught the standard; the rubrics will tell students how well they mastered the standard. The road from standards to rubrics is paved with challenges, but when the journey ends, students, parents, teachers, and administrators have to admit, *"Rubrics are our friends!"*

RUBRIC CHECKLIST

Application

Assignment: Review your rubric and self-assess your final product.

Did you include the following criteria?	Not Yet 0	Some Evidence 1
Headings:		
• Title of item being assessed ("Rubric for Oral Presentation")		
• State standard/benchmark number and key words (Language Arts Standard 6.5, *"Speaking to persuade"*)		
• Place for student's name, period, course, or grade level		
• Place for date of assessment		
Scoring Levels:		
• Four levels ranging from one to four (even numbers only)		
• Zero is understood for no evidence of effort		
• The highest score of "4" sets clear expectations of what students must do to exceed standards ("A" work)		
• Scoring levels include number ("1") and description ("Novice")		
• Scoring levels could include pictures that describe levels		
Descriptors/Elements or Indicators:		
• The umbrella criterion ("Organization") should not be graded; the indented bullet points ("Introduction," "Body") should be graded		
• The descriptors are concise and specific (avoid words/phrases like "some," "few," "adequate," "good," "most of the time")		
• The descriptors should use the vocabulary from the state standards as well as synonyms from the textbook		
• Some criteria can be weighted ("Organization × 4")		
Format:		
• Use graphics and pictures to add visual appeal		
• Tally each criterion on the side to get a score (Analytical Rubric)		
• Total each criterion score to arrive at a final score		
• Provide a scale to convert rubric score to final grade		

Scale:
15–17 = A
13–14 = B
10–12 = C
Not Yet

Final Grade: _____

Figure 6.13

CREATE A RUBRIC

Application

Goals/Standards: _____

Assignment: Select a group or individual checklist and convert it to a rubric

SCALE:	1	2	3	4
CRITERIA:				
[ ] •				
•				
•				
[ ] •				
•				
•				
[ ] •				
•				
•				
[ ] •				
•				
•				

Figure 6.14

Burke, K. (2005). *How to Assess Authentic Learning,* 4th Ed. Thousand Oaks, CA: Corwin Press. Used with permission.

DESIGN TEACHING RUBRICS

Reflection

Step 6: Design Teaching Rubrics

How good is good enough? How can students attain excellence by achieving the indicators described in the rubric?

1. How do checklists differ from rubrics?

2. Why do students need to see a rubric prior to completing a project or performance?

3. Why can we say "Rubrics are our friends!"?

Figure 6.15

CHAPTER 7

FINAL THOUGHTS

A new role for assessment has been emerging over the past decade, in which assessment is viewed as a tool that can inform instruction, improve student achievement, and ultimately provide more and better education for the learner.

—Asp (2001, p. 508)

Teaching is a challenging profession in today's high-stakes accountability environment. Many veteran teachers lament the loss of spontaneity and creativity in the classroom. They feel that the increased emphasis on standards and standardized tests has limited their time for integrating long-term projects and in-depth units into their lesson plans. They remember the days when weeks could be spent studying the Civil War or a novel like *The Diary of Anne Frank,* allowing the students the freedom to branch off into other related topics that piqued their interest. Whether they finished everything in the five-inch-thick county curriculum guide was of little consequence. The students were motivated, and they were involved in their own learning. The students may have missed out studying other wars and other novels, but they would probably retain what they did learn. Besides, rarely did anyone ever keep track of what a teacher did or did not address, and end-of-the-course tests or standardized tests to measure a student's yearly progress did not exist. Moreover, many teachers the next school year would spend 2 to 3 weeks reviewing what students should have learned the previous year.

Conversely, many teachers who started teaching in the past 5 years may not have experienced the freedom and autonomy of "self-pacing" and/or "teacher-selected curriculum." They joined the profession during the era of the scarlet letter A, for accountability! Many of these educators received scope and sequence pacing guides, the state standards, curriculum guides, test-preparation booklets, benchmark test dates, *No Child Left Behind* booklets, a schedule of professional development sessions devoted to performance assessment, workshops on how to differentiate the needs of all learners, and checklists to monitor when each standard was introduced and when each child mastered the standard. It was, to paraphrase Dickens, the best and worst of times. On a 1 to 4 scale, with 1 focusing on traditional teaching and standardized testing and 4 describing differentiated teaching and standards-based assessment, teachers tend to self-assess themselves at "somewhere in the middle" or "too close to retirement to care!"

Assessment, like diets and budgets, needs to be balanced. The balanced assessment model that integrates traditional teaching and testing, portfolio or work samples, and performance tasks and projects meets the needs of the national mandates, state accountability, and the students. The in-depth motivating unit that the students love still has its place in the curriculum—as long as the content, concepts, and standards are embedded in the unit. Similarly, when a teacher spends too much time on one unit, the students may not receive the fundamental skills or other important content pieces they need to know in order to be successful in other courses, college, or life. Moreover, although students may have "loved" the engaging unit that lasted 6 weeks, they may fail to appreciate what they learned if they fail the district's end-of-course tests, the state test, the ACT, SAT, or any achievement tests required for admission to the college of their choice. Teachers, therefore, must balance their instructional time to prepare students for the problem-solving challenges of life as well as the high-stakes tests that determine promotion, scholarships, and access to higher education.

A balanced assessment program offers students multiple opportunities to show what they know through tests, portfolios, projects, and performances. The program provides multiple assessments to showcase their multiple intelligences. Striking the appropriate balance for each student is a critical challenge for all teachers in the twenty-first century. Teachers do make a difference. By targeting the standard, finding the big ideas, organizing teacher checklists, creating performance tasks, designing student checklists, and developing teaching rubrics, teachers embed the knowledge and skills from the standards in engaging and relevant lessons that motivate all students to learn.

Costa and Kallick (2001) discuss how success depends on gathering information from a variety of feedback sources in order to analyze, interpret, and internalize the data. Once the data are analyzed, individuals and organizations can modify their actions to achieve the goals. "Thus, individuals—and the organization—are continually self-learning, self-renewing, and self-modifying." (p. 524). By using a repertoire of curriculum designs, instructional strategies, and performance assessments, teachers prepare students to be successful in their classes, on standardized tests, and in their daily lives. Assessment guides instruction when it is used as a tool to inform instruction, improve student achievement, and provide a positive learning experience for all students.

RESOURCE A: THE GREATEST BOOK EVER

A Kindergarten Rhyming Words Unit

The Greatest Book Ever

A Kindergarten Rhyming Words Unit

Unit: Rhyming Words	Time Frame: Three Weeks	Grade/Subject: Kindergarten—Language Arts

Primary State Standards

Phonological Awareness Kindergarten Language Arts—The student demonstrates the ability to identify and orally manipulate words and individual sounds within those spoken words.

Secondary State Standards

Language Arts—The student begins to understand the principles of writing.
Language Arts—The students uses oral and visual skills to communicate.
Language Arts—The student gains meaning from orally presented text.

Big Ideas:

How families/rhyming words are made.
How illustrations must coincide with the rhyming words and student sentences.

Essential Questions:

Why is it important to listen?

How can you tell if a word rhymes with another?

How can you tell rhyming/word family words apart from other words?

How will learning rhyming/word family words help you read more efficiently?

The Greatest Book Ever

A Kindergarten Rhyming Words Unit

Standard: Language Arts—The student demonstrates the ability to identify and orally manipulate words/individual sounds within those spoken words.

Task Description:

Listen everyone! Dr. Seuss needs our help in writing his next book. He needs our help in thinking up new and fun rhymes to make this his "Greatest Book Ever." He heard about all the work we've been doing on making up rhyming words that make sense and our creative nonsense rhyming words. He saw our writing/pictures in our blending syllables books we made earlier this month. Dr. Seuss needs our ideas and examples (as many as we can) in a book by the end of this month so he can read it to other kids to see how they like it. He then wants to have it in our stores by the holiday season.

Direct Instruction for Whole Class: The whole class will be involved in the following learning experiences:

- Students will listen to, look through, and discuss other Dr. Seuss books.
- Students will locate rhyming words in various types of literature.
- Teacher will record student responses on nonsense rhyming words and rhyming words that make sense.
- Students will work together to create sentences using rhyming words/blends to use high-frequency words in their sentences (use chart paper).

Group Work:

Group One
Create rhyming word sentences.

Group Two
Create poster to notify primary grades to come hear Dr. Seuss read his new book.

Group Three
Illustrate pages for class book.

Group Four
Design a title and cover for the class book.

Individual Work:

- Each child will create a page for the class book.
- Each child will create an illustration using his or her own rhyming words.
- Each child will record his or her favorite Dr. Seuss books and his or her three favorite rhymes.

Methods of Assessment:

- Checklists
- Rubrics
- Observation
- Journal Writing

Checklist for Page in Class Book

Class Book Page Checklist

Standards: Language Arts—The students will use oral and visual skills to communicate. Language Arts—Demonstrate the ability to identify and orally manipulate words/sounds.

Assignment: Create a Dr. Seuss rhyming word class book page

Criteria/Performance Indicators		
Content: Does your page have . . .?		
• *your name on the page*		
• *the date on the page*		
• *a rhyming word sentence*		
• *a picture*		
Mechanics: Grammar		
• *Did you add space between words?*		
• *Did you start new sentences with a capital letter?*		
• *Did you end with the correct punctuation?*		
Visual Effects		
• *Is your writing neat?*		
• *Does your picture have 3 or more colors?*		
Resources		
• *Did you list your 3 favorite Dr. Seuss books?*		
• *Did you list your 3 favorite rhyming words?*		
Delivery to Class		
• *Did you practice saying your sentence?*		
• *Can you explain your picture?*		
• *Do your sentence and picture go together?*		

Student sign: _____

Teacher sign: _____

Parent sign: _____

Comments: _____

Total Smiles: _____

13–14 GREAT

10–12 Good Job

0–9 Keep Working

Class Book Page Rubric

Activity: Individual Rhyming Word Class Book Page

Language Arts Standards: Use oral and visual skills to communicate, identify, and orally manipulate words or sounds.

SCALE: CRITERIA:	1 Below the Standard	2 Approaching the Standard	3 Meets the Standard	4 Exceeds the Standard
Content • Name	Scribbles	Correct but uses all upper/lower-case	First letter is a capital letter; others are lowercase	First and last name is correct
• Date	Scribbles	Uses numbers but incorrect	Correct date	Wrote out month
• Sentence	Scribbles	Labels or uses random letters	Sentence makes sense	Sentence is grammatically correct
Mechanics • Proper spacing	No spacing	Spacing but inappropriate places	Space between each word	
• Capitalization	All letters same size	Random capital letters	Correct words capitalized	
• Punctuation	No punctuation	Incorrect punctuation	Correct punctuation	
Visual Effects • Neatness	Scribbling and crossing out	Some scribbling	Nice handwriting	Great penmanship
• Illustration	Scribbles	Picture doesn't go with sentence	Picture coincides and is recognizable	No problem recognizing all pictures
Resources • 3 Dr. Seuss books	0	1	2	3
• 3 rhyming words	0	1	2	3

Class Book Page
Rubric (Continued)

Activity: Individual Rhyming Word Class Book Page

Language Arts Standards: Use oral and visual skills to communicate, identify, and orally manipulate words or sounds.

SCALE:	1	2	3	4
CRITERIA:	Below the Standard	Approaching the Standard	Meets the Standard	Exceeds the Standard
Delivery • Speaking	Won't talk at all	Will talk but not on topic	Reads sentence correctly	Reads sentence with personality
• Picture Explanation	Scribbles, but can't tell about it	Draws picture but it doesn't go with sentence	Clear explanation of picture	Adds descriptive details
• Coincide Picture/ Sentence	No picture or no sentence	Has both, but they do not coincide	Picture and sentence coincide	Explains the connection between picture and sentence

Unit created by Krista L. Drescher of DeKalb County Schools, Decatur, Georgia. Used with permission.

RESOURCE B: SHOWCASE OF AMERICAN HEROES

A First-Grade Social Studies/Language Arts Unit

Showcase of American Heroes

A First-Grade Social Studies/Language Arts Unit

Unit: American Heroes	Time Frame: Six weeks	Grade/Subject: First Grade—Social Studies/ Language Arts

Primary State Standards: The student will read about and describe the lives of historical figures in American history. The student will identify the contributions made by these figures: Thomas Jefferson (Declaration of Independence), Meriewether Lewis and William Clark with Sacajawea (exploration), Harriett Tubman (Underground Railroad), Theodore Roosevelt (national parks and environment), George Washington Carver (science), Benjamin Franklin (inventor/author/statesman).

Secondary State Standards:

Social Studies:

1. The student reads about and describes the lives of historical figures in American history.

2. The student describes how the *everyday* life of these historical figures is similar to and different from *everyday* life in the present (e.g., food, clothing, homes, transportation, communication, recreation).

Language Arts:

1. The student begins to demonstrate competency in the writing process.

2. The student writes in complete sentences with correct subject-verb agreement.

3. The student begins to use common rules of spelling.

4. The student begins to use a variety of resources (e.g., picture dictionaries, the Internet, books) and strategies to gather information to write about a topic.

5. The student uses appropriate end punctuation (e.g., period, question mark) and correct capitalization of initial words and common proper nouns (e.g., personal names).

6. The student uses oral and visual strategies to communicate.

Science:

1. The student will communicate scientific ideas and activities clearly.

Art:

1. The student will draw pictures (grade-level appropriate) that correctly portray features of the person, place, event, or object being described.

Big Idea:

The students will be able to identify and describe the lives of historical figures in American history and appreciate their contributions to American life.

Essential Questions:

- Why could George Washington Carver be called a "nutty" professor?
- How do we use Dr. Carver's inventions today?
- How is Benjamin Franklin "electrifying?"
- Why was Harriet Tubman's "railroad" a secret?
- What do our neighborhood park and Theodore Roosevelt have in common?
- Where did Sacajawea lead Meriwether Lewis and William Clark, and how did they get there?
- Why could July 4th be called "Thomas Jefferson" day?

American Heroes Unit

First Grade

Subject Areas: Social Studies, Language Arts, Science, and Art Standards

Task Description:

The local Museum of History is just too full! It only has space to showcase one additional great American hero in its American History wing. The museum board members don't know what to do and they desperately need your help! Because of your vast knowledge of historical figures, they would like you to decide which one of these figures deserves this prestigious spot. Your work will convince the museum board which additional American historical figure belongs in the museum. To convince the museum directors, each group will create a poster display board and a model or artifact for Benjamin Franklin, Thomas Jefferson, Lewis and Clark with Sacajawea, Harriet Tubman, Theodore Roosevelt, or George Washington Carver. The museum board members will visit our classroom on October 15 to judge your poster and model; they will select the hero who belongs in the space they have left. Put on your historical hero hardhats and get to work! You're the experts, and the museum board is counting on you.

Direct Instruction for Whole Class:

The whole class will be involved in the following learning experiences:

- Class discussion about contributions of the six historical figures
- Biographical books and/or videos presented to students on each hero
- Classroom Venn diagram created to compare and contrast *food, clothing, homes, transportation, communication,* and *recreation* of the past and present for the heroes
- Class project on making peanut butter

Group Work:

Each group will create a poster display board and a model or artifact that represents one historical figure's contributions to American History. Students may select their group.

Group One:	Group Two:	Group Three:	Group Four:	Group Five:	Group Six:
Benjamin Franklin	*Thomas Jefferson*	*Lewis and Clark with Sacajawea*	*Harriet Tubman*	*Theodore Roosevelt*	*George Washington Carver*

Individual Work:

Each student will create his or her own *American Heroes* book. In the book, each student will be expected to:

– name *all six of the people studied,*
– name their contribution,
– provide at least two illustrations for each hero, and
– write a complete sentence about each historical figure.

Methods of Assessment:

- Checklist for each group poster display board, model, or artifact
- Checklist and rubric for each student's individual *American Heroes* book
- Teacher observation and teacher-made tests

Group Work Checklist

Name: _____   Date: _____   First-Grade Social Studies

Display Poster Boards for Heroes

Standard: Read about and describe the life of historical figures in American history.

Checklist: Display poster boards for six American heroes—group work.

Criteria/Performance Indicators	Not Yet 0	Some Evidence 1
Content		
• Does your poster have a title?		
• Did you include the historical figure's first and last names?		
• Did you include a picture of the historical figure?		
• Did you include the historical figure's birthday?		
• Did you include the historical figure's contributions in your three sentences?		
• Does your project include a model? My model is _____.		
Mechanics		
• Did you use common rules of spelling?		
• Did you use correct capitalization?		
• Did you use correct punctuation?		
Appearance		
• Is your poster 18" by 24"?		
• Did you use at least *three* colors on your poster?		
• Is your poster neat and free of smudges?		

Reflection:

Student's Signature: _____

Teacher's Signature: _____   Final Grade: _____

Grading Scale
S: 11–12
N: 9–10
U: 0–8

American Heroes Book Checklist

Name: _____   Date: _____   First-Grade Social Studies

Standard: Social Studies, Language Arts, Science, Art

Individual Work: *American Heroes* book

Criteria/Performance Indicators	Not Yet 0	Some Evidence 1
Content		
• Does your book have a cover?		
• Does your cover have a title?		
• Did you include your name on the cover?		
• Does each historical figure have a whole page?		
• Did you include the first and last names of all *six* historical figures?		
• Did you provide at least *two* illustrations of the contributions of each historical figure?		
• Did you write at least *one* complete sentence for each historical figure?		
Mechanics		
• Did you use common rules of spelling?		
• Did you use correct capitalization?		
• Did you use correct punctuation?		
Appearance		
• Did you use at least *three* colors in your book?		
• Is your book neat and free of smudges and erasures?		
• Did you staple your booklet together?		

> **Grading Scale**
> S: 11–13
> N: 9–10
> U: 0–8

Student's Signature: _____

Teacher's Signature: _____   Final Grade: _____

American Heroes Book Rubric

Individual Assignment:	Each student will create his or her own *American Heroes* book. In the book, each student will be expected to list any six of the people studied and their contribution, provide at least two illustrations for each hero, and write a complete sentence about each historical figure.
Goal/Standard:	Social Studies: The student will read about and describe the life of historical figures in American history.

Criteria	1 Below the Standard	2 Approaching the Standard	3 Meets the Standard	4 Exceeds the Standard
Cover: • Has a cover • Cover has a title • Name on the cover	Includes 1 of the criteria	Includes 2 of the criteria	Includes all 3 criteria	• Includes all 3 criteria • Illustrations
Content: • Has first and last name of 6 historical figures • Named at least 2 contributions for each historical figure • Provided at least 2 illustrations for each historical figure • Included at least 1 complete sentence for each historical figure	Includes 1 or 2 of the criteria	Includes 3 criteria	Includes all 4 criteria	• Includes all 4 criteria • Additional interesting fact for each historical figure
Mechanics: • Used common rules of spelling • Used correct capitalization • Used correct punctuation	Includes 1 of the criteria	Includes 2 of the criteria	All 3 criteria	• All 3 criteria met • Words spelled correctly

Appearance: • Used at least 3 colors in your book • Book is neat and free of smudges and erasures • Book is stapled together	Includes 1 of the criteria	Includes 2 of the criteria	Includes all 3 criteria	• Includes all 3 criteria • Cover is the front page • Pages are numbered and in order

Grading Equivalents:

S = 12–16 points; N = 8–11 points; U = 0–7 points.

Student Signature: _____   **Total Score:** _____

Teacher Signature: _____

Unit created by Juanita Nelson, Jacinta Alexander, Jacqueline Burns, LaTrece Crane, Lydia Rice, and Elijah Swift. Fulton County Board of Education. Tri-Cities/Banneker Cluster, Atlanta, GA. Used with permission.

RESOURCE C:
REVAMPING
"OLD GLORY"

A Second-Grade Social Studies/Reading Unit

Revamping "Old Glory"

A Second-Grade Social Studies/Reading Unit

Unit: The American Flag	Time Frame: 2 weeks	Grade/Subject: Second—Social Studies/Reading

Primary State Standards:

Social Studies—Citizenship: Describes proper flag etiquette including handling, display and disposal of flag; explains the significance of the stars, stripes, and colors.

Social Studies—Information Processing: Acquires information through reading, observing, and listening.

Research—Information Processing: Uses various sources to locate information.

Reading—Vocabulary: Reads and uses new words in oral and written language.

Reading—Comprehension: Reads for information; summarizes text content; makes connections.

Secondary State Standards:

Social Studies—Information Processing: Arranges events, facts, and ideas in sequence.

Social Studies—Civic Participation: Works within groups.

Vocabulary: Uses oral language to inform and entertain.

Reading—Fluency: Reads with expression.

Writing: Uses organizational patterns (chronological order, similarities/differences); uses transitional words and phrases; uses a variety of resources.

Math—Problem Solving: Employs problem-solving strategies.

Math: Adds 1-, 2-, and 3-digit numbers with and without regrouping.

Big Ideas:

The importance of citizenship and civic responsibility in a free society.
How symbols represent countries and patriotism.

Essential Questions for the Unit:

What is the purpose of a flag?

How do flags symbolize patriotism?

How can flags help improve school spirit?

How does the American Flag represent our country?

Revamping "Old Glory"

Learning Standard: Social Studies—Citizenship: The student describes proper flag etiquette including handling, display, and disposal of flag and explains the significance of the stars, stripes, and colors.

Task Description:

A new state has joined the United States of America and the current flag must be replaced. You have been selected by the federal government to enter a contest to design a new flag that would include the new state. In order to convince government officials to use your design, you must demonstrate your expertise in the significance of the stars, stripes, and colors as well as proper flag etiquette by:

1. developing a visual timeline of all American flags from past to present;

2. researching and creating a PowerPoint presentation on the history of the American Flag;

3. writing and performing a skit describing proper flag etiquette;

4. preparing a brochure that explains the significance of the stars, stripes, and colors of the American Flag;

5. calculating the cost to make and ship a new jumbo flag to the White House, a new large flag to each state capital, and a new small flag to schools and businesses.

Be prepared to present your entry to the officials next week when they judge the finalists.

Direct Instruction for Whole Class:

The whole class will be involved in the following learning experience:

1. Class discussion on the significance of the stars, stripes, and colors of the American Flag.

2. A video detailing the proper handling, display, and disposal of the flag.

3. Flag-folding demonstration by safety patrols.

4. Small-group project: Venn diagram of the similarities and differences between one past flag and the current flag.

5. A review of the formats of various brochures.

Group Work:				
Group One	**Group Two**	**Group Three**	**Group Four**	**Group Five**
Develop a visual timeline of the flags from past to present	Research and create a PowerPoint presentation on the history of the American Flag	Write and perform a skit describing proper flag etiquette	Prepare a brochure that explains the significance of the stars, stripes, and colors of the American Flag	Calculate the cost to make and ship a new jumbo flag to the White House, a new large flag to each state capital, and a new small flag to schools and businesses in our community

Individual Work:

1. Create a new American flag that includes the newly added state.

2. Create a brochure that explains proper flag etiquette.

Methods of Assessment:

1. Teacher-made test

2. Checklists for each group assignment

3. Checklist and rubric for individual work

4. Journal for self-reflection

Checklist for Flag Picture and Brochure

Standard: Social Studies—Citizenship: Describes proper flag etiquette including handling, display, and disposal of flag and explains the significance of the stars, stripes, and colors.

Criteria/Performance Indicators	Not Yet 0	Some Evidence 1
Flag Content		
• Did you use the colors red, white, and blue?		
• Did you include stars to represent the states?		
• Did you include stripes to represent the colonies?		
Flag Appearance		
• Is your flag 8½" x 11"?		
• Is your flag neat and free of smudges?		
Brochure Cover		
• Did you include a title?		
• Did you include a picture?		
• Did you include your first and last name?		
• Did you include the date?		
• Did you include your teacher's name?		
• Did you include your grade level?		
Brochure Content		
• Did you include instructions for properly *handling* the flag?		
• Did you include instructions for properly *displaying* the flag?		
• Did you include instructions for properly *disposing* of the flag?		
• Did you include three vocabulary terms?		
• Did you include transitional words?		
• Did you use at least two different sources?		

Checklist for Flag and Brochure (Continued)

Criteria/Performance Indicators	Not Yet 0	Some Evidence 1
Mechanics		
• Did you use common rules of spelling?		
• Did you use correct capitalization?		
• Did you use correct punctuation?		
Appearance		
• Did you include at least three pictures?		
• Did you type your brochure?		
• Did you fold the brochure properly?		
• Is your brochure neat and colorful?		

Student Comment: _____   Total Points: [ ]

Teacher Comment: _____

Grading Scale
18–24 = A
13–17 = B
07–12 = C

Rubric for Flag Picture and Brochure

Standard: Social Studies—Citizenship: Describes proper flag etiquette including handling, display, and disposal of flag and explains the significance of the stars, stripes, and colors.

Flag Picture and Brochure	1 Below the Standard	2 Approaching the Standard	3 Meets the Standard	4 Exceeds the Standard	Score
Flag Content • Includes red, white, and blue? • Includes stars for states? • Includes stripes for colonies?	Includes 1 of the criteria	Includes 2 of the criteria	Includes 3 of the criteria	• Includes all 3 • Is creative • Is visually appealing	
Flag Appearance • Is 8½" x 11"? • Is neat • Is free of smudges?	Includes 1 of the criteria	Includes 2 of the criteria	Includes 3 of the criteria	• Includes all 3 criteria • Is visually appealing	
Brochure Cover • Includes title? • Includes picture? • Includes first and last names? • Includes date? • Includes teacher's name? • Includes grade level?	Includes 1-2 of the criteria	Includes 3-4 of the criteria	Includes 5-6 of the criteria	• Includes all 6 of the criteria • Creative • Visually appealing	
Brochure Content • Includes instructions for handling? • Includes instructions for displaying? • Includes instructions for disposing?	Includes 1 of the criteria	Includes 2 of the criteria	Includes 3 of the criteria	• Includes all 3 criteria • Creative • Visually appealing	
• Includes vocabulary terms?	Includes 1	Includes 2	Includes 3	Includes 4 or more	
• Includes transitional words?	Includes 1	Includes 2	Includes 3	Includes 4 or more	
• Uses different sources?	Includes 1	Includes 2	Includes 3 or more	Current sources	

Rubric for Flag Picture and Brochure (Continued)

Flag Picture and Brochure	1 Below the Standard	2 Approaching the Standard	3 Meets the Standard	4 Exceeds the Standard	Score
Mechanics • Correct spelling? • Correct capitalization? • Correct punctuation?	Includes 5 or more errors	Includes 3-4 errors	Includes 1-2 errors	Contains no errors	
Appearance • Includes pictures? • Is typed? • Is folded properly? • Is neat and colorful?	Includes 1 of the criteria	Includes 2 of the criteria	Includes 3 of the criteria	Includes all 4 of the criteria	

Grade Equivalents:

27–36 = A; 18–26 = B;
9–17 = C; 16 or below = NOT YET!

Final Grade: _____

Comments:

Total Points: [   ]

Created by Gillian B. Conner, LaTanja M. Harris, June Ladson, and LaSonya M. Magee in a workshop for DeKalb County Schools, Decatur, GA. Used with permission.

RESOURCE D: OUR GOVERNOR WANTS YOU!

A Third-Grade Social Studies/Language Arts Unit

Our Governor Wants You!

A Third-Grade Social Studies/Language Arts Unit

Unit: State Government	Time Frame: 3 to 4 weeks	Grade/Subject: Third Social Studies/ Language Arts

Primary State Standards:

Social Studies: Students explain the difference between making laws, carrying out laws, and determining if laws have been violated; students also identify the governmental bodies that perform these functions at the local, state, and national levels.

Writing: Students begin to select a focus and an organizational pattern based on purpose, genre, expectations, audience, and length.

Focus of This Unit: State government

Secondary State Standards:

Social Studies: Describes how violations of law produce consequences.

Social Studies: Identifies the current governor as leader of state.

Social Studies: Explains the rules and laws that protect an individual's rights.

Social Studies: Uses print and nonprint reference sources to locate information.

Social Studies: Illustrates data in a variety of graphic forms.

Big Idea:

The three branches of state government work together to create, carry out, and interpret laws that protect the rights of people. The balance of power among them prevents any of the three branches from becoming too strong—"Checks and Balances."

Essential Questions for the Unit:

Why do we need laws and government?

How do they protect us?

What would life be like if we did not have laws?

What happens when people break laws?

How are laws created in a democracy?

Why do we have three branches of government and a system of checks and balances?

What are our responsibilities as citizens in helping to create laws and in obeying them?

Our Governor Wants You!

Learning Standard: Social Studies: Students identify the state governmental bodies that make laws, carry out laws, and determine if laws have been violated.

Task Description: The governor of our state wants you! The Chinese ambassador is planning a visit to our state's capitol building, and the governor wants our class (with its prodigious knowledge of state government) to be his sidekicks as he guides the ambassador through the capitol. To be chosen, you must all be able to:

- Explain the structure and operation of the three branches of state government using display boards as visual aids;
- Participate in a role-play that demonstrates the formation, passage, and interpretation of laws;
- Sing the "I'm Just a Bill" song from the DVD *School of Rock*.

Be prepared to join our governor when he welcomes our new friends from China on _____.

Direct Instruction for Whole Class: The whole class will be involved in the following learning experiences:

- Participation in introductory class discussion of the three branches of state government.
- Presentation of group research and display boards.
- Learning the song "I'm Just a Bill."
- Acting as a member of the legislative, executive, or judicial branch of state government in class, role-play about the interaction of the branches.
- Reviewing the components of letter writing.

Group One: Research the *duties* of the *legislative* branch	**Group Two:** Research the *duties* of the *executive* branch	**Group Three:** Research the *duties* of the *judicial* branch
Group Four: Research current *officials* of *legislative* branch	**Group Five:** Research current *officials* of *executive* branch	**Group Six:** Research current *officials* of *judicial* branch

Group Work: Students work in groups of two or three to (1) do Internet research on the three branches of state government and our current officials, and (2) create display boards as visual aids.

Groups combine to create display boards: groups one and four; groups two and five; groups three and six.

Individual Work: Each student writes a letter to a pen pal in China describing in detail the structure and operation of the state government. In each letter, the student will describe the three branches of government and how laws are created, upheld, and interpreted. The student will also incorporate all components of effective letter writing.

Methods of Assessment:

- Checklist for group research projects and presentations
- Teacher observation of group participation
- Checklist and rubric for letters to pen pals

Our Governor Wants You!
Checklist for Pen Pal Letter

Standard: Students identify the state governmental bodies that create, enforce, and interpret laws.

Checklist: Organization and content of letter to pen pal.

Criteria/Performance Indicators	Not Yet 0	Some Evidence 1
Paragraph 1: Introduction:		
• Did you introduce yourself?		
• Did you tell your pen pal where you live?		
• Did you tell your pen pal your age, grade, and the name of your school?		
• Did you tell your pen pal why you are writing to him or her?		
Paragraph 2: Introduction of Content		
• Did you capture your reader's attention by using a lead (i.e., grabber, hook)?		
• Did you name the 3 branches of government?		
• Did you include at least 3 sentences?		
Paragraph 3: Executive Branch Content		
• Did you begin with a transition word or phrase?		
• Did you describe the responsibilities of the executive branch?		
• Did you list the current officials and their titles?		
• Does your paragraph contain at least 5 sentences?		
Paragraph 4: Legislative Branch Content		
• Did you begin with a transition word or phrase?		
• Did you describe the responsibilities of the legislative branch?		
• Did you list the current officials and their titles?		
• Does your paragraph contain at least 5 sentences?		
Paragraph 5: Judical Branch Content		
• Did you begin with a transition word or phrase?		
• Did you describe the responsibilities of the judicial branch?		

Checklist for Pen Pal Letter (Continued)

Criteria/Performance Indicators	Not Yet 0	Some Evidence 1
• Did you list the current officials and their titles?		
• Does your paragraph contain at least 5 sentences?		
Paragraph 6: Checks and Balances Content		
• Did you begin with a transition word or phrase?		
• Did you describe how the 3 branches work together and balance their power?		
• Does your paragraph contain at least 4 sentences?		
Paragraph 7: Conclusion		
• Did you begin with a transition word or phrase?		
• Did you reiterate (repeat) your reason for writing?		
• Did you conclude with a friendly, personal sentence?		
• Does your paragraph contain at least 3 sentences?		
Letter Format		
• Did you write the *date* at the top of your letter?		
• Did your letter have a *salutation*?		
• Did your letter have a *body*?		
• Did your letter have a *closing*?		
• Did your letter have your *signature*?		

Student Comment: _____

Teacher Comment: _____

Total Points

[ ]

(out of 31)

Scale:

27–31 = A
23–26 = B
19–22 = C
Not Yet

Final Grade: _____

Our Governor Wants You!
Rubric for Pen Pal Letter

Assignment: Students write letters to pen pals in China, describing our state government.

Goal/Standard: Social Studies: Students describe the functions of the three branches of state government and the system of checks and balances.

SCALE CRITERIA:	1 Below the Standard	2 Approaching the Standard	3 Meets the Standard	4 Exceeds the Standard
Paragraph 1 • Introduction • Where you live • Age, grade, school • Reason for writing	Includes 1 or 2 of the criteria	Includes 3 of the criteria	Includes all 4 of the criteria	Includes all 4 of the criteria and written in correct form
Paragraph 2 • Lead • Names of 3 branches • 3 or more sentences	Includes 1 of the criteria	Includes 2 of the criteria	Includes all 3 of the criteria	Includes all 3 of the criteria with a motivating lead
Paragraph 3 • Transition • Duties of executive branch • Officials and titles • 5 or more sentences	Includes 1 or 2 of the criteria	Includes 3 of the criteria	Includes all 4 of the criteria	Includes all 4 of the criteria with extensive information and creative expression
Paragraph 4 • Transition • Duties of legislative branch • Officials and titles • 5 or more sentences	Includes 1 or 2 of the criteria	Includes 3 of the criteria	Includes all 4 of the criteria	Includes all 4 of the criteria with extensive information and creative expression

Rubric for Pen Pal Letter (Continued)

SCALE	1	2	3	4
CRITERIA:	**Below the Standard**	**Approaching the Standard**	**Meets the Standard**	**Exceeds the Standard**
Paragraph 5 • Transition • Duties of legislative branch • Officials and titles • 5 or more sentences	Includes 1 or 2 of the criteria	Includes 3 of the criteria	Includes all 4 of the criteria	Includes all 4 of the criteria with extensive information and creative expression
Paragraph 6 • Transition • Interaction of 3 branches • 4 or more sentences	Includes 1 of the criteria	Includes 2 of the criteria	Includes all 3 of the criteria	Includes all 3 of the criteria with thorough explanation of balance of power
Paragraph 7 • Transition • Reason for writing restated • Friendly, personal sentences • 3 or more sentences	Includes 1 or 2 of the criteria	Includes 3 of the criteria	Includes all 4 of the criteria	Includes all 4 of the criteria with an excellent reason for writing
Letter Formats • Date • Salutation • Body • Closing • Signature	Includes 1 or 2 of the criteria	Includes 3 of the criteria	Includes 4 of the criteria	Includes all 5 of the criteria spelled and punctuated correctly

Grading Equivalents:

A = 28–32;   B = 24–27;   C = 19–23.

Total Points: _____

(out of 32)

Unit created by Lara McMahan, Brenda Avery, and Janice Alvarez in a workshop for DeKalb County Schools, Decatur, GA. Used with permission.

RESOURCE E: SLAM DUNK! SCORING POINTS WITH THE NBA/WNBA

A Fourth/Fifth-Grade
Mathematics Unit

Slam Dunk! Scoring Points
With the NBA/WNBA:

A Fourth/Fifth-Grade Mathematics Unit

Unit:	Time Frame:	Grade/Subject:
Statistics and Probability	3 weeks	Fourth/Fifth Mathematics

Primary State Standards:

Mathematics Standards: The student will explore the concepts of mean and median. The student will collect, read, interpret, and compare data from charts, tables, and graphs (i.e., pictographs, bar graphs, and circle graphs) using a variety of scales and estimation.

Secondary State Standards:

Language Arts: The student will write in a variety of genres to produce paragraphs and compositions.

Technology: The student will utilize PowerPoint presentations to convey information.

Big Idea:

The students will be able to understand how to use statistics and probability skills to solve real-life problems related to mathematics and how to present accurate information to an outside audience.

Essential Questions for the Unit:

- What is the difference between mean and median?
- How do you calculate the mean and/or median of a set of numbers?
- How can collected data be analyzed and compared?
- What are the best methods to present data to illustrate the information?
- How do we use different types of writing to communicate ideas?
- How can we use technology to present data clearly and accurately?
- How can you evaluate the success of a basketball team and predict its future success as a franchise?

Slam Dunk! Scoring Points
With the NBA/WNBA

A Fourth/Fifth-Grade Mathematics Unit

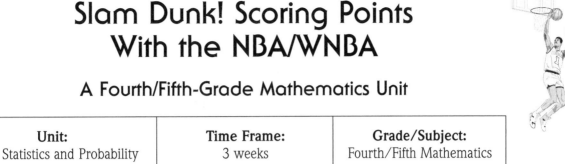

Unit:	Time Frame:	Grade/Subject:
Statistics and Probability	3 weeks	Fourth/Fifth Mathematics

Learning Standard: Math—The student explores the concepts of mean and median. Math—Collects, reads, interprets, and compares data from charts, tables, and graphs (i.e., pictographs, bar graphs, and circle graphs) using a variety of scales and estimation.

Task Description: The NBA and WNBA are in a bind! The statisticians for their best teams including the Los Angeles Lakers, the Detroit Pistons, the Indiana Pacers, the Minnesota Timber Wolves, the Charlotte Sting, the Los Angeles Sparks, the Washington Mystics, and the Detroit Shock have all quit and gone to work for casino mogul Donald Trump. The season is starting soon, and neither the NBA nor WNBA has been successful in hiring statisticians for these positions. Because of your knowledge of statistics and probability, the commissioners for the NBA and WNBA have chosen you to become one of their new statisticians for the upcoming basketball season. The project will include four tasks: (1) creating a booklet of the final scores for the past 3 years; (2) creating a PowerPoint presentation that displays the scores from the past 3 years; (3) writing an action plan to improve the team's performance and scoring; (4) making a graph of the scores from the past 3 years.

DUE DATE: _____

Direct Instruction for Whole Class: The whole class will be involved in the following learning experiences:

- Watching an NBA/WNBA basketball game on video or television
- Reviewing how to calculate mean and median
- Training in creating a PowerPoint presentation
- Reviewing places to find sources of information
- Reviewing the different types of graphs and their uses
- Training in the use of Internet search engines

Group Work: Students may select one of the following groups:

Group One	Group Two	Group Three	Group Four
Create a booklet of the final scores for the past 3 years including each game of the season and the average number of points scored per year.	Create a PowerPoint presentation that displays the scores from each game of the past 3 years with average yearly scores.	Write an action plan to improve the team's performance and scoring for the upcoming season.	Make a graph of the scores from the past 3 years that displays the team's scoring record and the average points for each year.

Individual Work: In addition to group work, all students will:

1. Write a paragraph describing your favorite professional basketball team's season (e.g., LA Lakers, Detroit Pistons, Philadelphia 76ers) based on the mean of the scores from one season and the players' statistics.

2. Create a chart that displays all the scores of your favorite team for the past 2 years.

Methods of Assessment:

- Checklist
- Rubric
- Teacher-made test on mean and median
- Group reflection paper describing participation and contributions

Checklist for Individual Paragraph

Unit: Statistics and Probability	Time Frame: 3 weeks	Grade/Subject: Fourth/Fifth Mathematics

Standard: Math—Explores the concepts of mean and median. Math—Collects, reads, interprets, and compares data from charts, tables, and graphs (pictographs, bar graphs, and circle graphs) using a variety of scales and estimation. Math—Write in a variety of genres to produce paragraphs and compositions.

Assignment: Write a paragraph describing your favorite professional basketball team's season (e.g., LA Lakers, Detroit Pistons, Philadelphia 76ers) based on the mean of the scores from one season and the players' statistics. Create a chart that displays all the scores of your favorite team for the past 2 years.

Criteria/Performance Indicators	Not Yet 0	Some Evidence 1
Accuracy of information:		
• Did you calculate the mean of the scores?		
• Did you find the median of the scores?		
• Did you use the Internet to locate an NBA/WNBA team?		
• Did you cite the Internet Web site?		
Organization:		
• Do you have a title?		
• Does your paragraph have an introduction or topic sentence?		
• Do you have at least 5 supporting sentences?		
• Did you use transition words?		
• Do you have a concluding statement?		

Mechanics:		
• Did you use complete sentences?		
• Did you use correct spelling?		
• Did you use correct grammar?		
• Did you use capital letters properly?		
• Did you adhere to rules of proper punctuation?		
Visuals:		
• Do you have a title or heading?		
• Is your information relevant to the topic?		
• Is your presentation attractive and neat in appearance?		
• Did you use correct size poster board (at least 24" × 26")?		
• Is your presentation colorful?		
• Did you organize your information into a chart?		

Student Comments: _____   **Total Points:** _____

Grading Scale: A (18–20); B (15–17); C (12–14); Below 12 (Not Yet)

Final Grade: _____

Student Signature: _____

Teacher Signature: _____

Slam Dunk! Scoring Points
With the NBA/WNBA

Rubric for Paragraph Assignment: Write a paragraph describing your favorite professional basketball team's season (e.g., LA Lakers, Detroit Pistons, Philadelphia 76ers) based on the mean of the scores from one season and the statistics of the players. Create a chart that displays all the scores of your favorite team for the past 2 years.

Goal/Standard: Math—Explores the concepts of mean and median.
Math—Collects, reads, interprets, and compares data from charts, tables, and graphs (i.e., pictographs, bar graphs, and circle graphs) using a variety of scales and estimation.

Scoring Criteria	1 You're Looking for Employment	2 The Local Government Might Hire You	3 The NBA/WNBA Will Hire You	4 The NBA/WNBA Will Love You!	Score
Accuracy of Information • Mean • Median • Web Sites Referenced	3 errors (mean, median, and incorrect citation)	2 errors (mean, median, or incorrect citation)	1 error (mean, median, or incorrect citation)	Mean and median are accurate. Information correct and cited in footnotes	___ × 10 ___ (40)
Organization • Title • Topic Sentence • Transitions • Conclusions	1 correct element	2 correct elements	3 correct elements	All elements present and organized in a coherent and eloquent manner	___ × 9 ___ (36)
Support Sentences (5)	1–2 support sentences	3–4 support sentences	5 support sentences	5 support sentences with a variety of sentence structures	___ × 2 ___ (8)
Mechanics: Correct Use of • Spelling • Grammar • Capitalization • Punctuation	5 or more errors	3–4 errors	1–2 errors	All elements correct	___ × 2 ___ (8)

Scoring Criteria	1 You're Looking for Employment	2 The Local Government Might Hire You	3 The NBA/WNBA Will Hire You	4 The NBA/WNBA Will Love You!	Score
Visuals • Title/Heading • Relevant information • Attractive and neat in appearance • Used correct size poster board (24" × 28") • Colorful	1 element present • *You're fired!*	2–3 elements present • *Take your resume to the employment office!*	4 elements present • *You're next in line for the job!*	All 5 elements present • Visually stimulating • Captivating to audience • *You're hired!*	___ × 2 ___ (8)

Student Comments:

Total: _____
(out of 100)

Teacher Comments:

Unit created by Delores Hall, Cynthia Bennett, Martha Williams, Serena Lowe, and Montreal Gore of Conley Elementary School. Fulton County Board of Education. Tri-Cities/Banneker Cluster, Atlanta, GA. Used with permission.

RESOURCE F: BOMBS AWAY . . . WORLD WAR II UNIT

Fifth-Grade Social Studies/ Language Arts Unit

Bombs Away . . . World War II Unit

A Fifth-Grade Social Studies/Language Arts Unit

Unit: World War II	Time Frame: 4 weeks	Grade Subject: Fifth-Grade Social Studies/ Language Arts

Primary State Standards: Social Studies:

- Analyze and explain major causes and effects of World War II
- Analyze and explain major events of World War II
- Identify and analyze World War II personalities

Secondary State Standards: Language Arts:

- Write a narrative essay
- Use proper conventions of grammar and punctuation

Big Idea:

The students will understand the political, economic, and social effects of World War II on the world and understand how key people influenced major events during the war.

Textbooks and Additional References:

- *Social Studies—The United States in Modern Times*—Harcourt Brace
- *The 20th Century by Sterling and Herwick*—Teacher Created Materials, Inc.
- *The Best of Mailbox Magazine—Exploring Social Studies*–Grades 4-6
- *Encyclopedia of the United States at War by English and Jones*—Scholastic, Inc.
- *World War II, Primary Sources Teaching Kit, Grades 4–8* by Sean Price—Scholastic, Inc.
- *World War II by* Tom McGowen—Franklin Watts
- *Highlights in American History, from 1850 to the Present* by Grace Kachaturoff—Frank Shaffer Publications
- *Inside the Hindenburg* by Majoor and Marschall—Madison Press

Essential Questions for the Unit:

- How did the events of WWII impact the world?
- Why do nations go to war?
- How does war impact the future?
- How do the actions of key people influence events before, during, and after a war?

Bombs Away . . .
World War II Unit

Title/Topic: <u>World War II</u>   Grade Level/Subject: <u>Fifth Grade</u>

Social Studies/Language Arts Performance Task

Standard/Benchmarks: Fifth-Grade Social Studies

- Analyzes and explains major causes and effects of World War II
- Analyzes and explains major events of World War II
- Identifies and analyzes World War II personalities

Task Description:

Your class has been selected as the designers of a new World War II Memorial Museum for young adults. While there have been many temporary exhibits, this will be the first permanent World War II Museum in our city that is especially designed for young adults. This task is an enormous responsibility that was bestowed upon your class because of your obvious expertise and creativity. For opening day, you will have to prepare the following:

1. A newspaper from the time period;
2. A PowerPoint presentation of major personalities;
3. A battleground brochure to be taken as a souvenir;
4. A skit of President Truman on trial for his actions regarding Hiroshima and Nagasaki.

Every task needs to be completed by opening day for the museum on: _____
Have fun and good luck with this important task!

Whole-Group Instruction:

- Create a KWL Graphic Organizer Chart showing what students know about World War II, what they want to find out, and what they have learned at the end of the unit
- Listen to textbook chapters on World War II curriculum tapes. Engage in class discussions
- Introduce key vocabulary associated with World War II
- Listen to lectures by teacher and take notes using graphic organizer (e.g. web or mind map)
- Brainstorm name for museum

Small Groups: Selected by Students: (Variety of multiple intelligences)

Group One	**Group Two**	**Group Three**	**Group Four**
Create a newspaper from the time period	Make a PowerPoint presentation of personalities	Design a Battle Ground Brochure	Write and perform a mock trial putting Truman on trial for Hiroshima and Nagasaki

Individual Work: Each student will complete the following:

1. Write a narrative account about World War II using a story starter provided by the teacher.
2. Create individual timelines of events, personalities, etc., from 1939–1945.

Methods of Assessment:

- Teacher-made test
- Criteria checklist for each group presentation
- Checklist and rubric for student narrative

Narrative Account Checklist

Criteria/Performance Indicators	Not Yet 0	Some Evidence 1
CONTENT:		
• Is the title related to the topic?		
• Did you use at least 3–5 facts from your resources:		

o Teacher provided resources
  o Textbook
  o Student group projects
  o Research materials		

• Does your narrative focus around 1 or more major events from the following choices:		

o Witness of the bombing of Pearl Harbor
  o American soldier in Europe on VE Day
  o Japanese citizen on VJ Day
  o Prisoner or Nazi soldier in Holocaust
  o Japanese American during Japanese internment		

FORMAT/ORGANIZATION:		
Introduction: Did you:		
• Use a hook/lead-in?		
• Establish the setting?		
• Introduce main character(s)?		
Middle/Body paragraphs: Did you provide:		
• Topic sentences?		
• 3–5 supporting sentences?		
• Closing sentence?		
Closing Paragraph: Does it:		
• Reflect on the impact of the paper's major event?		
Mechanics: Did you:		

• Apply standard rules for:
  o Spelling
  o Punctuation
  o Capitalization
  o Complete sentencing		

Bombs Away . . . Narrative Account Rubric

Criteria	Indicators	1 Lazy Larry	2 Mistaken Mary	3 Average Alvin	4 Hannah the Historian	Score
Mechanics	• *Spelling* • *Punctuation* • *Capitalization* • *Complete Sentences*	7 or more errors interfere with the reading of the paper	4–7 errors; interfere with the reading of the paper	3–6 errors; does not interfere with the reading of the paper	0 errors	___ out of 4
Organization	• Topic sentence for each paragraph	None	Topic sentence introduces some paragraphs	Topic sentence introduces all paragraphs	Topic sentence clearly introduces all paragraphs	___ out of 4
	• 3–5 supporting sentences per paragraph	Sentences that do not relate to the topic	1–2 supporting sentences	3–5 supporting sentences	5 or more supporting sentences that demonstrate connections	___ out of 4
	• Indenting	None	Incorrect use of indentation	Most paragraphs indented correctly	All paragraphs indented correctly	___ out of 4
Focus	• Centered around 1 event • 1 topic per paragraph	Student rambles off topic	Student occasionally gets off topic, but does choose 1 overall event	Student stays on topic in each paragraph and has an overall event focus	Each paragraph concisely focuses on its topic	___ out of 4
Style	• Point of view taken consistently throughout the paper	No point of view is chosen	Writes from more than 1 point of view	Writes from the chosen point of view	Writes from the chosen point of view and develops the character fully	___ out of 4
Content	• Hook	No hook	Hook doesn't get attention	Hook gets attention	Hook captivates audience	___ out of 4
	• Key people involved in narrative	Includes no people	Includes people	Includes people and titles	Includes people with titles and significance	___ out of 4
	• Paraphrase information effectively	Plagiarism	Some paraphrasing	Evidence of paraphrasing throughout with simple language	Evidence of paraphrasing throughout with effective language	___ out of 4

Criteria	Indicators	1 Lazy Larry	2 Mistaken Mary	3 Average Alvin	4 Hannah the Historian	Score
Content	• Accurate reporting of the events	Information not accurate	1–2 mistakes in reporting factual information	All factual information is accurate	Information accurate with examples and significance. In-depth research evident	___ out of 4

Final Grade: ____/40 or ____%

Student Reflections:

Unit created by Elaine Bolton, Margaret Breiner, Robyn Brown, Katie Byrd, Wendy Lea, Anita Lindsley, and Mae Maddox of the North Springs Assessment Cluster, Fulton County, Atlanta, GA. Used with permission.

RESOURCE G: SHUTTLE SAVERS

The Scientific Method Revisited—A Seventh-Grade Science Unit

Shuttle Savers

The Scientific Method Revisited

A Seventh-Grade Science Unit

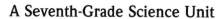

Unit: Scientific Method	Time Frame: Two weeks on 90-minute block schedule	Grade/Subject: Seventh-Grade Science

Primary State Science Standards:

- Ask quality questions
- Suggest reasonable hypothesis for identified problem
- Develop procedure(s) for solving problem
- Analyze scientific data
- Develop reasonable conclusion based on data collected
- Write clearly

Secondary State Standards:

- Suggest reasonable hypothesis for identified problem
- Develop procedure(s) for problem solving
- Ask quality questions
- Analyze scientific data

Big Idea:

The scientific method is a systematic procedure used to investigate and to solve scientific problems.

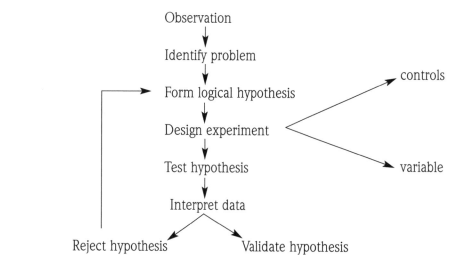

Essential Questions for the Unit:

How can the shuttle's design save lives?
How can a hypothesis be valuable when it turns out to be only partially accurate?

Shuttle Savers
The Scientific Method Revisited

Learning Standard: Students will identify and investigate problems scientifically.

Task Description: WNCS, our local news station, has just received a news flash from NASA announcing that the shuttle Odyssey 2X has been destroyed. The director of NASA needs your help to find the cause of this disaster. NASA officials are debating the cause. Some officials strongly believe terrorists are involved while others think a meteorite struck the shuttle. Mechanical engineers believe that it was destroyed as a result of a malfunction in the design of the shuttle. Can your class help them solve this problem? If your classes are successful, you will be the dinner guests of former astronaut John Glenn and receive special awards at the White House to honor your contributions to science and the United States space program.

Direct Instruction for Whole Class: The whole class will be involved in the following learning experiences:

- Brief lecture on the scientific method
- Class discussion on space shuttle tragedies, past and present
- Viewing of *Apollo 13* movie that describes the scientific method used by NASA to solve problems
- Field trip to the NASA center in Huntsville, AL
- Readings from textbook, nonfiction books, and periodicals

Group Work:

Group One	**Group Two**	**Group Three**	**Group Four to Six**
NASA officials are exploring the possibility that terrorists may be the cause of the disaster. NASA is asking for your help. Your job is to examine the possibility that terrorists could have done this.	Some scientists believe that a meteorite may have caused the disaster. They need your help. Your job is to determine whether this could have occurred.	NASA officials fear that a flaw in their own design could have contributed to the loss of life. They have asked your help in establishing whether the shuttle design could have been the determining factor.	Students will brainstorm and research ideas to design a space shuttle that they believe to be flawless, considering that terrorists (group 1), a meteorite (group 2), or a design flaw (group 3) may have been the culprit.

Individual Work: Each student will create a review booklet containing:

1. A cover page with related title and illustration

2. A summary of each group's findings

3. An analysis and critique of each group's work

4. Student's own hypothesis as to what caused the tragedy

5. Commentary on what may avert future disasters

Methods of Assessment:

1. Checklist for each group project

2. Checklist and rubric for individual booklet

3. Teacher observation

4. Teacher informal talk(s) with group

5. Teacher-made test

Scientific Review
Booklet Checklist

Standard: Shuttle Savers: The Scientific Method Revisited-Checklist

Criteria/Performance Indicators	Not Yet 0	Some Evidence 1
Cover Page		
• Title		
• Picture		
• Name and date		
• Class period		
Summary of Group's Findings		
• Group One		
• Group Two		
• Group Three		
• Group Four		
• Group Five		
• Group Six		
Critique of Group's Findings		
• Group One		
• Group Two		
• Group Three		
• Group Four		
• Group Five		
• Group Six		
Formation of Own Hypothesis		
• Feasible		
• Logical		
• Supporting arguments		

Mechanics		
• Spelling		
• Punctuation		
• Topic and closing statements		
• Supporting sentences		

Grading Scale:
A 21–23
B 18–20
C 15–17

Total Points: _____
(23)

Final Grade: _____

Student Comments:

Student Goal for Next Assignment:

Teacher Comments:

Parent Comment:

Brochure Rubric

Assignment: Shuttle Savers Brochure

Goal/Standard: Students will identify and investigate problems scientifically.

Scoring Criteria	1 Scrubbed Mission	2 Grounded	3 Lift-Off	4 In Orbit	Score
Cover page – title-picture – name/date/class – period	0 out of 3	1 out of 3	2 out of 3	3 out of 3	___ × 5 ___ (20)
Summaries – main idea – conciseness – data-problem defined	0 out of 3	1 out of 3	2 out of 3	3 out of 3 Problem clearly defined	___ × 5 ___ (20)
Critiques – conciseness – logical – supporting statements – reflections	1 out of 4	2 out of 4	3 out of 4	4 out of 4	___ × 5 ___ (20)
Hypothesis – logical – supporting arguments	Not logical	Logical with 1 supporting argument	Logical with 2 supporting arguments	Logical with 3 supporting arguments	___ × 5 ___ (20)
Mechanics – spelling – punctuation – topic statement – closing statement	1 out of 4	2 out of 4	3 out of 4	4 out of 4 Flawless mechanics	___ × 5 ___ (20)

Score
A = 90–100
B = 80–89
C = 71–79
D = 70

Final Score: _____

(100)

Final Grade: _____

Comments: _____

Created by Gloria Winslow Smith, Christopher Chambers, and Dr. Teri Williams in a workshop for DeKalb County Schools, Decatur, GA. Used with permission.

REFERENCES

Amrein, A. L., & Berliner, D. C. (2003). A research report: The effects of high-stakes testing on student motivation and learning. *Educational Leadership, 60*(5), 32–38.

Arter, J., & McTighe, J. (2001). Scoring rubrics in the classroom: Using performance criteria for assessing and improving student performance. In T. R. Guskey & R. J. Marzano (Eds.), *Experts in Assessment.* Thousand Oaks, CA: Corwin Press.

Asp, E. (2001). To think or not to think: Thinking as measured on state and national assessments. In A. L. Costa (Ed.). *Developing minds: A resource book for teaching thinking* (3rd ed., pp. 497–510). Alexandria, VA: Association for Supervision and Curriculum Development.

Baker, B., Costa, A., & Shalit, S. (1997). The norms of collaboration: Attaining communication competence. In A. Costa & R. Liebmann (Eds.), *The process-centered school: Sustaining a renaissance community* (pp. 119–142). Thousand Oaks, CA: Corwin Press.

Barell, J. (2003). *Developing more curious minds.* Alexandria, VA: Association for Supervision and Curriculum Development.

Black, P., Harrison, C., Lee, C., Marshall, B., & Wiliam, D. (2004). Working inside the black box: Assessment for learning in the classroom. *Phi Delta Kappan, 86*(1), 8–21.

Bransford, J., Brown, A. L., & Cocking, R. R. (Eds.). (2000). *How people learn: Brain, mind, experience, and school.* Washington, DC: National Academy Press.

Brooks, J. G. (2002). *Schooling for life: Reclaiming the essence of learning.* Alexandria, VA: Association for Supervision and Curriculum Development.

Burke, K. (2005). *How to assess authentic learning* (4th ed.). Thousand Oaks, CA: Corwin Press.

Burke, K., Fogarty, R., & Belgrad, S. (2002). *The portfolio connection: Student work linked to standards* (2nd ed.) Thousand Oaks, CA: Corwin Press.

Carr, J. F., & Harris, D. E. (2001). *Succeeding with standards: Linking curriculum, assessment, and action planning.* Alexandria, VA: Association for Supervision and Curriculum Development.

Conzemius, A., & O'Neill, J. (2001). *Building shared responsibility for student learning.* Alexandria, VA: Association for Supervision and Curriculum Development.

Costa, A. L., & Kallick, B. (2004a). *Assessment strategies for self-directed learning.* Thousand Oaks, CA: Corwin Press.

Costa, A. L., & Kallick, B. (2004b). Launching self-directed learners. *Educational Leadership, 62*(1), 51–55.

Costa, A. L., & Kallick, B. (2001). Building a system for assessing thinking. In A. L. Costa *Developing minds: A resource book for teaching thinking* (3rd ed., pp. 517–524). Alexandria, VA: Association for Supervision and Curriculum Development.

Danielson, C. (2002). *Enhancing student achievement: A framework for school improvement.* Alexandria, VA: Association for Supervision and Curriculum Development.

Danielson, C. (1996). *Enhancing professional practice: A framework for teaching.* Alexandria, VA: Association for Supervision and Curriculum Development.

Depka, E. (2001). *Designing rubrics for mathematics: Standards, performance tasks, checklists, student-created rubrics.* Thousand Oaks, CA: Corwin Press.

Donne, J. (1623). Meditation 17. *Devotions upon emergent occasions, XVII.*

Drake, S. M., & Burns, R. C. (2004). *Meeting standards through integrated curriculum.* Alexandria, VA: Association for Supervision and Curriculum Development.

DuFour, R. (2004). What is a "professional learning community"? *Educational Leadership, 61*(8), 6–11.

Fogarty, R., & Pete, B. (2005). *Differentiated learning: An anthology to reach and teach all students.* Chicago, IL: Fogarty & Associates.

Gardner, H. (1993). *Multiple intelligences: The theory in practice.* NY: Basic Books.

Gentile, J. R., & Lalley, J. P. (2003). *Standards and mastery learning: Aligning teaching and assessment so all children can learn.* Thousand Oaks, CA: Corwin Press.

Georgia Department of Education's Quality Core Curriculum. (2004). Georgia Department of Education.

Goodlad, J. I. (1994). *A place called school. Prospects for the future.* New York: McGraw-Hall.

Graham, B. I., & Fahey, K. (1999). School leaders look at student work. *Educational Leadership, 56*(6), 25–27.

Gronlund, N. E. (1998). *Assessment of student achievement* (6th ed.). Boston: Allyn & Bacon.

Guastello, E. F. (2004, May). *A village of learners.* Alexandria, VA: Association for Supervision and Curriculum Development.

Guskey, T. R. (2003). How classroom assessments improve learning. *Educational Leadership, 60*(5), 7–11.

Guskey, T. R. (2001). Helping standards make the grade. *Educational Leadership, 59*(1), 20–27.

Guskey, T. R., & Bailey, J. M. (2001). *Developing grading and reporting systems for student learning.* Thousand Oaks, CA. Corwin Press.

Hunter, M. (1971). *Transfer*. El Segundo, CA: Tip. In *Differentiated learning: Different strokes for different folks*, Fogarty, R., 2001.

Intrator, S. M. (2004). The engaged classroom. *Educational Leadership, 62*(1), 20–24.

Jerald, C. D. (2001). Dispelling the myth revisited: Preliminary findings from a nationwide analysis of high-flying schools. In R. D. Barr & W. H. Parrett, *Saving our students, saving our schools* (pp. 27–31). Thousand Oaks, CA: Corwin Press.

Lewin, L., & Shoemaker, B. J. (1998). *Great performances: Creating classroom-based assessment tasks*. Alexandria, VA: Association for Supervision and Curriculum Development.

Littky, D. (2004). *The big picture: Education is everyone's business*. Alexandria, VA: Association for Supervision and Curriculum Development.

Little, J. W., Gearhart, M., Curry, M., & Kafka, J. (2003). Looking at student work for teacher learning, teacher community, and school reform. *Phi Delta Kappan, 85*(3), 185–192.

Marshall, K. (2003). A principal looks back: Standards matter. *Phi Delta Kappn, 85*(20), 105–113.

Martin-Kniep, G. O. (2000). *Becoming a better teacher: Eight innovations that work.* Alexandria, VA. Association for Supervision and Curriculum Development.

Marzano, R. J. (2003). *What works in schools: Translating research into action.* Alexandria, VA: Association for Supervision and Curriculum Development.

Marzano, R. J. (2000). *Transforming classroom grading.* Alexandria, VA: Association for Supervision and Curriculum Development.

Marzano, R. J., Kendall, J. S., & Gaddy, B. B. (1999). *Essential knowledge: The debate over what Americans should know.* Aurora, CO: Mid-Continent Research for Education and Learning.

Marzano, R. J., Marzano, J. S., & Pickering, D. J. (2005). *Classroom management that works: Research-based strategies for every teacher.* Upper Saddle River, NJ: Prentice Hall.

McMillan, J. H. (2001). *Essential assessment concepts for teachers and administrators.* Thousand Oaks, CA: Corwin Press.

McTighe, J., & Thomas, R. S. (2003). Backward design for forward action. *Educational Leadership, 60*(5), 52–55.

McTighe, J., & Wiggins, G. (1999). *The understanding by design handbook.* Alexandria, VA: Association for Supervision & Curriculum Development.

Meier, D. (2002). Standardization versus standards. *Phi Delta Kappan, 84*(3), 190–198.

Nelson, K., & Lindley, K. (2004). *Starting strong: Surviving and thriving as a new teacher.* Thousand Oaks, CA: Corwin Press.

Newman, F. M. (1996). *Authentic achievement: Restructuring schools for intellectual quality.* San Francisco, CA: Jossey-Bass.

Nitko, A. J. (2001). *Educational assessment of students* (3rd ed.). Upper Saddle River, NJ: Prentice Hall.

Popham, W. J. (2003). *Test better, teach better: The instructional role of assessment.* Alexandria, VA: Association for Supervision and Curriculum Development.

Popham, W. J. (1999). *Classroom assessment: What teachers need to know* (2nd ed.). Boston: Allyn & Bacon.

Reeves, D. B. (2004). *Accountability for learning: How teachers and school leaders can take charge.* Alexandria, VA: Association for Supervision and Curriculum Development.

Roy, P. (2004a, October). Begin with the end in mind. *Results.* Oxford, OH: National Staff Development Council.

Roy, P. (2004b, November). The three elements of the standards. *Results.* Oxford, OH: National Staff Development Council.

Saddler, B., & Andraode, H. (2004). The writing rubric. *Educational Leadership, 62*(2), 48-52.

Sagor, R. (2003). *Motivating students and teachers in an era of standards.* Alexandria, VA: Association for Supervision and Curriculum Development.

Schmoker, M. (2004). Tipping point: From feckless reform to substantive instructional improvement. *Phi Delta Kappan, 85*(6), 424–432.

Schmoker, M. (2002). Up and away—Lifting low performance. *National Staff Development Council, 23*(2), 10–13.

Schmoker, M. (2001). *The results fieldbook: Practical strategies from dramatically improved schools.* Alexandria, VA: Association for Supervision and Curriculum Development.

Sheldon, K. M., & Biddle, B. J. (1998). Standards, accountability, and school reform perils and pitfalls. *Teachers College Record, 100*(1), 164–180.

Solomon, P. G. (2002). *The assessment bridge, positive ways to link tests to learning, standards, and curriculum improvement.* Thousand Oaks, CA: Corwin Press.

Solomon, P. G. (1998). *The curriculum bridge: From standards to actual classroom practice.* Thousand Oaks, CA: Corwin Press.

Sousa, D. A. (1995). *How the brain learns.* Reston, VA: The National Association of Secondary School Principals.

Stiggins, R. J. (2002). Assessment crisis: The absence of assessment for learning. *Phi Delta Kappan, 83*(10), 758–765.

Stone, R. (2001). *How teachers can assess the thinking skills they are teaching.* In A. Costa, (Ed.) *Developing minds: A resource book for teaching thinking* (3rd ed., pp. 525–527). Alexandria, VA. Association for Supervision and Curriculum Development.

Storz, M.G., & Nestor, K. R. (2003). Insights into meeting standards from listening to the voices of urban students. *Middle School Journal, 34*(4), 11–19.

Strong, R.W., Silver, H. F., & Perini, M. J. (2001). *Teaching what matters most: Standards and strategies for raising student achievement.* Alexandria, VA: Association for Supervision and Curriculum Development.

Tomlinson, C. A. (2003). *Fulfilling the promise of the differentiated classroom: Strategies and tools for responsive teaching.* Alexandria, VA: Association for Supervision and Curriculum Development.

Tomlinson, C. A. (1999). *The differentiated classroom: Responding to the needs of all learners.* Alexandria, VA: Association for Supervision and Curriculum Development.

Tomlinson, C. A., & Edison, C. C. (2003). *Differentiation in practice: A resource guide for differentiated curriculum Grades 5–9.* Alexandria, VA: Association for Supervision and Curriculum Development.

Wiggins, G. (1998). *Educative assessment: Designing assessments to inform and improve student performance.* San Francisco, CA: Jossey-Bass.

Williams, B. (Ed.). (1996). *Closing the achievement gap: A vision of changing beliefs and practices.* Alexandria, VA: Association for Supervision and Curriculum Development.

Wolfe, P. (2001). *Brain matters: Translating research into classroom practice.* Alexandria, VA: Association for Supervision and Curriculum Development.

Zmuda, A., Kuklis, R., & Kline, E. (2004). *Transforming schools: Creating a culture of continuous improvement.* Alexandria, VA: Association for Supervision and Curriculum Development.

INDEX